INVESTMENT STRATEGIES UNDER CLINTON/GORE

Learn how to maximize
your money in these changing
and unpredictable times.

Gordon K. Williamson

Williams
PUBLISHING

 Published in the United States by Williams Publishing, Inc., PO BOX 3006, Portland Oregon 97208

ISBN: 0-9635289-2-0

First Edtion

Printed in the United States Of America

9 8 7 6 5 4 3 2

You may contact Gordon Williamson at:

1-800-748-5552

Table of Contents

Introduction

We enter an era marked with a mandate; no other Democratic president in the past 45 years has won by such a wide margin, both in the electoral college and popular vote, as Clinton (Johnson's victory was greater, but he ran as an incumbent). As President Clinton settles into office as the leader of the only remaining super power in the world, the big question for you, the investor, is: Where should you invest your money? Should you make radical changes? Is a defensive posture the right course of action, or will select risk-taking result in some tremendous profits?

In addition to answering these broad-based questions, this book provides some very specific investment information such as:

1. Whether domestic investments will outperform their foreign counterparts.
2. Whether you should favor stocks over bonds.
3. The outlook for real estate, particularly personal residences.
4. Which industries to look at and which areas of corporate America to avoid.

5. If securities are part of your portfolio, whether individual issues are a better choice than mutual funds.
6. How to build a financial plan for the next 4–8 years.
7. The changes in store for income taxes.

The information in this book can be tailored to meet your particular needs, fears, hopes, and concerns. Once armed with the needed answers to the issues raised above, you will see exactly which stocks, bonds, real estate, and mutual funds are right for you.

The difference between Clinton and Bush is extreme; however, the contrast between Clinton and Reagan is not. While campaigning in 1987 and after taking office in 1988, George Bush made it very clear that the Reagan second-term agenda would continue: Make no major changes; let the economy continue to run on its own steam. In 1990, a senior staff member for the administration declared that Congress could go home for the next two years; that there was no more meaningful legislation to pass during the remainder of what was thought to be Bush's *first* term. At the time, this seemed like a good idea. After all, Bush had been involved in administrations that had experienced the greatest uninterrupted post-war economic boom the country had seen in over half a century.

Bill Clinton has taken a Reagan-like approach: Make the first couple of hundred days count. Be determined that this presidency will begin with a running start. Although not a big fan of Reagan's *entire* tenure, President Clinton has publicly stated that he admires Reagan's skills in quickly and decisively dealing with Congress. And, despite a series of battles and compromises, Clinton realizes that Reagan's first year set the tone for the balance of his first term. Such single-mindedness resulted in Reagan getting most of his personal agenda passed. Bill Clinton plans on doing the same thing.

After losing his first bid for re-election as governor, Clinton had time to reflect on his leadership abilities. The loss ended up being beneficial, both for Clinton then, and the American people now. Then Governor Clinton realized that the best way to govern was to concentrate on a few key issues and work hard for legislation in those specific areas. It was this political education that helped lead him to the presidency, and it will be this insightful leadership that will help this country.

Investment Overview

To be successful in making your investment, tax, and estate-planning decisions for the next few years you always need to be cognizant of President Clinton's three priorities:

1. Job creation accomplished by economic growth through government stimulus.
2. A delayed deficit reduction plan that will go into effect once the economy starts to flourish.
3. An attack on medical costs that will result in a comprehensive health care program intended to cover every US citizen.

As you will see later, each of these points creates opportunities for you as well as potential pitfalls if you do not closely follow the road map included here.

You will find investment opportunities in corporations that are in the business of training people. One of the President's first priorities will be to provide more training and apprenticeships for the non-college bound. And, although you cannot benefit from this, it is also likely that financially strapped students wishing to attend college will get loans in return for two years of national service.

Another area important to the President is civilian research and development (R & D) and infrastructure projects such as roads, bridges, fiber-optic networks, and high-speed rail systems. As an investor, you can benefit from such projects, and help the country, by investing in the common stocks of companies that provide the labor, materials, plans, and consulting services for such ventures.

Despite an initial deficit increase of approximately $50 billion, long-term rates will initially go lower. Short-term rates will stay where they are or rise modestly for the following reasons:

- Clinton understands that he is *inheriting* an economy; his responsibility is not to reshape things immediately and make them work.
- Clinton is very sensitive politically and very smart.
- There is a need for moderate fiscal stimulus (adding $30–60 billion to the debt) that generates economic activity gradually.
- The economy is not likely to take off since there is no world economic locomotive (there is no indication that any major economic power has any policies in place that will help).
- Restructuring is not over; expect more layoffs in 1993 and 1994 (this restructuring will also take place in Japan and especially in Europe for a number of years).
- If Clinton tries enormous fiscal stimulus, the financial markets will bring about a slowdown in economic activity.
- There is less liquidity in the financial system than

there used to be, making it almost impossible to set off a wave of inflation (which in turn would hurt the bond market).

- Interest rates can go lower; *adjusted for inflation*, intermediate and long-term rates are now fairly high, around 3–3.5%.
- A rise in rates would be negative for equity markets, particularly the issuance of new shares, which in the past, were so beneficial in rehabilitating businesses, not to mention all of the money that would shift from equity mutual funds into higher yielding money market and bond funds.

The restructuring of federal government expenditures and receipts will help offset a good portion of the economic stimulus package planning by Clinton from a dollars and cents point of view as well as a pyschological one. Both are important concerns to the stock, bond, and real estate markets. This restructuring, which will add money to Federal coffers, includes:

- Cuts in defense and medicare.
- Tax on upper-income groups, which will increase demand for tax-exempt bonds and dividend-paying stocks (tax-frees still offer up to 90% the yield of comparable government bonds).
- Shifting the cost of certain federal programs to local governments and the private sector.

Congress won't act on Clinton's fiscal proposals until the second quarter of 1993. The impact after such action will not be immediate. Greenspan will remain as chairperson of the Fed; however, a number of the Federal Reserve governors may go back to private life. The Fed will almost certainly do something, such as lower the Federal Funds rate one more time. It can't afford to wait for Clinton's actions to pass and take hold. *Modest* economic growth in the 2-3% range is the key. A growth rate of 3.5–4% in real Gross Domestic Product (GDP)would cause chaos in the stock market due to expectations of higher interest rates and that such growth would not be sustainable.

The Economy

There may be pressure by the electorate for Clinton to act quickly to lower unemployment, but there is no quick fix because:

- Middle-management that is out of work needs to be retrained.
- Money is needed to rebuild the infrastructure.
- Government expenditures must be capped.

Perhaps the best answer is to lower taxes as a percentage of GDP and reduce regulations. The motivation will not be to balance the federal budget, but to pursue economic policies that will allow the US economy to grow faster than the debt accumulates. For the stock market, this uncertainty breeds investment opportunity. The economic environment will be characterized by continued slow growth, with quarterly spurts here and there, low inflation, and relatively low interest rates.

Remember, investing requires anticipation; to get value you must be ahead of the crowd. The economic situation today is very much like what existed prior to 1982. Equity investors will be well-advised to invest fixed amounts over regular periods in the months ahead to take advantage of the market's volatility (see the example of dollar-cost averaging in Chapter 6, *Small Cap Stock*).

Interest Rates

The Fed will allow rates to fall, but won't push them. The Federal Reserve Board has continued to ignore pleas from economists and politicians of both political parties to push interest rates down. The Fed's monetary policy is being guided by the markets rather than political or ideological considerations. This monetary policy should continue under this and future presidential administrations.

Taxes

It is estimated that passing an investment tax credit (ITC) alone will create at least 500,000 new jobs. Even though weekly new jobless claims continue to be in the 340,000–400,000 range, an ITC coupled with the optimism that a new presidency creates will be just the match needed to light the fuse to get Congress and the country moving again. As you see the new jobless claims fall, keep in mind that there is natural bottom, a figure of 300,000 new claims per week is what we have experienced during boom or expansionary periods.

Most people can concentrate on trying to make more money, either from their job or investments, but a small percentage of you will be paying more taxes. The top rate will go from 31% to 36–40%, there will be a surtax on annual incomes over $1 million, and a more punishing alternative minimum tax (which will hurt incomes that are largely sheltered by write-offs). Taxes that will affect most of us include raising costs to industrial polluters and the manufacturers of alcohol and tobacco. You will also be paying more for imported products. Foreign companies that have operations in the US, such as Nissan and Toyota, will collectively begin to pay several billion dollars a year in taxes.

According to some of the top financial publications, it will be best for you to consume during the first few years of a Clinton administration, later switching to investments. Some top Democratic and Republican leaders feel that the future lies in some type of consumption tax, similar to what Europe has had for several years in the form of a value-added tax (VAT). Although the deficit will increase during 1993 and 1994, President Clinton is serious about its reduction, and a consumption tax is one of his best options. It is doubtful that an ITC, infrastructure growth, and job training, paid for by a host of miscellaneous taxes, will be enough to cut the budget.

Surprisingly, when it comes to personal income taxes, it has been the Republicans that have soaked the rich, not the Democrats. Consider the following facts:

- Nixon raised the capital gains tax dramatically.
- Carter lowered the capital gains tax dramatically.
- Reagan eliminated almost all tax loopholes.
- Bush increased taxes.
- Clinton will increase taxes for those with incomes over $200,000 ($150,000 for people filing a single or individual return), but will include loopholes.

In short, the Democrats like high tax rates and lots of loopholes; the Republicans prefer lower top tax rates with fewer loopholes but the loopholes are always large. As an example, it was just a couple of years ago when Democratic Senator Moynihan successfully lobbied for the reinstatement of the full write-off of appreciated property to museums. For example, in the past, if you had a painting that you paid $20,000 for and it appreciated to $50,000, only a $20,000 write-off was allowed if the painting was donated. Because of the Democratic

Senator's efforts, the write-off is now $50,000 in this example.

While the American people may accept a somewhat liberal administration, they will not tolerate a tax-and-spend Congress. Tax policy will be a major focus of this discussion. Here are the tax issues most likely to dominate the discussion:

- Capital gains
- Retirement savings
- Corporate tax incentives
- Enterprise zones
- National sales tax.

President Bill Clinton says he wants to end the "cold war" between Congress and the White House. But he'll need help from the 121 new faces in the 103rd Congress—the most newcomers since 1948. The new members of Congress were polled after the election by *Money Magazine*. Here are the results:

- 96% of the new members polled favor liberalizing IRAS.
- 46% stated their own ideas about reforming health care, though almost half of the new Democrats like Clinton's plan to guarantee coverage for all.
- 95% want to lower the rate on capital gains, but in various ways.
- 33% would curb mortgage deductions or eliminate them for second homes.

A mere 10% said they would support curtailing entitlements, including Social Security. And just 13% would dare to even hike taxes on Social Security benefits that go to wealthy seniors.

By international standards, the claims on US taxpayers are modest.

Total Tax Revenue
(As a Percentage of GDP)

Japan	26%
US	**28%**
Canada	34%
U.K.	37%
Germany	39%
France	42%
Netherlands	48%
Sweden	49%

Real Estate

At the core of any meaningful recovery is real estate. New construction, along with all of the ancillary industries and companies that are affected by it, will be the key to a lasting recovery. If long-term interest rates do not fall, the health of the housing market is in serious condition. As an investor, you should stay clear of real estate during 1993 and 1994 unless you see the yield on the bellwether 30-year government bond drop to 7.25% or lower. If rates rise instead, avoid property and look to other investments that benefit from higher interest rates (see the following chapter, *Money Market Funds*).

Let us now move from the central themes and agenda that will be put into place over the next few years, to specific investments that will fare well under President Clinton.

1

Money Market Funds

IF YOU FEEL THAT interest rates are going to climb moderately or substantially during the Clinton years, there is no safer haven than a money market fund. You may not want to invest in government, municipal, or corporate bonds because when interest rates rise, bond values drop (if the bond is held until it matures, it will regain any such "paper losses" and can be redeemed for full face value). Rising interest rates often spell trouble for real estate and stocks. Yet, when rates go up, so do yields on money market funds.

It has only been since the early 1980's that the political parties have come to grips with the fact that, in the end, it is the capital markets that impose limits as to what is acceptable when it comes to the economy. If Clinton does not recognize this reality, money market funds will be one of the few certain benefactors. To gain a better perspective as to how the federal government has dealt with financial markets, review the past 30 years. Even though John Kennedy appointed a Wall Street insider as his first Treasury secretary (the head of Clinton's economic security council was, until his appointment, co-chairperson of Goldman, Sachs, & Co.), the president still regarded corporate America as a hostile force, viewed as being at odds with his progressive social initiatives.

Lyndon Johnson, in typical fashion, brow-beat his economic forecasters into making ridiculous growth assumptions, thereby concealing the true costs of the Vietnam War.

Richard Nixon ended the link between gold and the US dollar so that there would be less focus on inflation during his 1972 bid for reelection. His wage-and-price controls created a false sense of prosperity that soon turned into a major recession.

Gerald Ford and Jimmy Carter thought that oil-price increases could be hidden by simply printing more money. Reagan's tax cuts helped, but there was no second part to his plan: our debt expanded in an almost exponential manner. The final tab for this spending party was given to George Bush. Unable to get the public's mind off the burdening debt and the closely linked recession, Bush was not invited back for a second engagement.

Based on past history, it is no wonder that the financial markets are weary of any administration, Republican or Democratic; for it has been both parties that have been pro-debt, pro-inflation, or pro-anything that is likely to make things look good temporarily. So, if you see interest rates start to head up, sell your long-term bonds (in this case, any government or corporate bond with a remaining maturity of greater than 10 years), and put the proceeds in a money market fund at your local bank or brokerage firm, or with your favorite mutual fund group. Once rates level off or begin to drop, then look to other investment vehicles.

Since money market funds are being recommended as a shelter against higher interest rates, let us see how mutual funds work and, more specifically, see how money market accounts benefit while other investments tread water or begin to sink.

A *mutual fund* is an investment company that pools the money of many individual investors. When the fund takes in money from investors, it issues shares. Money market funds are simply one type of mutual fund. These funds invest in short-term money market instruments. By maintaining a short average maturity, usually less than 60 days, and investing in high-quality instruments, money market funds can maintain a stable $1 per share.

Since money market funds offer yields higher than insured bank money market deposit accounts, they are a very attractive haven for savings or temporary investment dollars. Money market funds come in both taxable and tax-free versions. Reflecting their tax-free status, municipal money market funds pay lower *before-tax* yields than taxable money market funds, but can offer higher returns on an *after-tax* basis.

Since the price per share of taxable money market funds always stays at $1, interest is shown by the accumulation of additional shares (for example, at the beginning of the year you may have 1,000 shares and by the end of the year 1,050, the 50 share increase, or $50, represents interest). There are no such things as capital gains or loses in a money market fund. The entire return, or yield, is fully taxable (except in the case of a tax-free money market fund where your "gain" or return would always be exempt from federal taxes and possibly state income taxes as well).

No one has ever lost a dime in a money market fund. These funds are designed as a place to park your money for a relatively short period of time, in anticipation of a major purchase (such as a car, house, furniture, or home remodeling) or until conditions appear more favorable for stocks, bonds, real estate, or a combination of the three.

Background

Money market funds revolutionized savings in America. Many of today's investors first encountered a mutual fund when they bought a money market fund. In the late 1970's and early 1980's, the interest rates that banks and thrifts could pay savers were set by bank regulators and they were kept artificially low. Those with $10,000 could pull their money out of the bank and buy Treasury bills (T-bills), but there was no high-interest vehicle for individuals with less money until the money market mutual fund.

These funds pooled investors' money and bought the kind of higher-yielding money market investments that individuals could not get on their own—such as Treasury bills, jumbo certificates of deposit, and commercial paper (short-term corporate IOUs). When short-term interest rates soared to almost 20% in the early 1980's, money market funds made it possible for anyone to cash in on the enormous yield.

Money market funds also resuscitated the mutual fund industry, which for years had been suffering from net redemptions. Simply put, investors were taking more money out of the funds than they were putting in. By 1982, money market funds had commandeered about $200 billion in assets. When the great bull market in stocks and bonds got underway, the mutual fund companies had millions of new customers to whom they could pitch their stock and bonds. Not only did money market fund investors start switching into stock and bond funds, they also brought in money from other sources. At year-end 1982, the mutual fund industry counted about $300 billion in assets. By 1985 it was nearly half a trillion, and today it stands well over $1.3 trillion.

Track Record

Historical returns over the past three, five, 10, and 15 years for T-bills (a substitute for money market funds) are shown as follows (for periods ending 11/30/92). All of the figures shown in the table are average *annual* rates of return.

Category	Years 3	5	10	15
T-bills	3.5%	5.6%	6.3%	8.2%
Rate of inflation (Consumer Price Index)	4%	4.2%	3.8%	—

As you can see, the returns on money market funds have not been particularly exciting over the past few years. During any period of time when interest rates are low, this investment will not turn in the kind of returns it experienced in the early and mid 1980's. And, since interest rates are expected to stay low for at least the next few years, you might ask, Why keep any money here at all?

One reason is safety. Since money funds invest in securities with maturities of a year or less, the risk of loss is minuscule. A second reason is convenience. Most money market funds offer free check-writing privileges. Also, if long-term rates surprise the experts by spurting upward, you can move a portion of your money fund holdings into longer-term funds to lock in higher earnings.

Summary

No matter how conservative an investor you are, or how certain you are that interest rates are going to go up, keep in mind two very important points. First, no one has successfully predicted interest rates over any meaningful period of time. In fact, trying to guess what interest rates will do next is as difficult as trying to figure out what the stock market will do tomorrow or next year. Second, the return (or yield) on money market funds, once adjusted for inflation and income taxes, has been negative two-thirds of the time over the past 20 years.

No investment plan or strategy should be without an exit, something safe to get into if everything seems to go awry. From a practical point, money market funds are an investment that should be part of everyone's portfolio, if for no other reason, as a temporary parking place to put money while contemplating other purchases or investments, or as a vehicle to be used to pay monthly bills.

The president campaigned on a commitment to stimulate the economy. The *conventional* ways to do that are to increase federal spending (for example, build highways and fix bridges), lower taxes, increase the deficit, and print more money. Tax rates will not be lowered, but it is almost a certainty that most, if not all, of these other measures described earlier in the chapter will be used. Done in moderation, the outcome can be quite positive. However, if you start to see the financial markets at odds with the president (such as stock or bond prices suddenly and persistently dropping), watch out. The markets do not like uncertainty. The only marketplace nimble enough to surely benefit short-term from such an environment will be money market instruments.

2

Municipal Bonds

As you learned from the summary in the last chapter, Bill Clinton's tools to stimulate the economy are limited. One point he has not been shy about has been the need to raise taxes. There will be no real relief for the middle class. The upper-middle class and truly wealthy will either be paying more taxes or looking for loopholes. However, since most loopholes were closed in the 1980's, one of the few remaining alternatives will be tax-free bonds.

There are few investments that perform well with higher tax rates, but municipal bonds do. If you are in a low tax bracket (or are thinking of ways to invest sheltered money in a retirement plan), you can still benefit from a tax-and-spend policy by buying common stock of companies such as Franklin, USAA, T. Rowe Price, and others who specialize in offering tax-free mutual funds and unit trusts.

Since you are probably not in the lowest tax bracket, read on. You will be surprised to learn that only a small percentage of those who can benefit from tax-free investing actually take advantage of it.

Municipals, also known as tax-free, are debt instruments issued by states, counties, districts, or political subdivisions. Interest from municipal bonds is normally exempt from federal income tax. In almost all states, interest is also exempt from state and local income taxes if the portfolio is made up of issues from the investor's state of residence, a US territory (such as Puerto Rico and the Virgin Islands), or the District of Columbia.

It is this tax-free status of municipals that makes them so attractive, particularly for high-income earners who now have higher tax rates to look forward to. Tax-free bonds, municipal bond funds, tax-free unit trusts, and tax-free money market funds are the only investments available that provide tax-free income without any strings attached. In later chapters you will discover investments or ways of obtaining tax-advantaged or tax-sheltered income, but all such vehicles have catches.

To fully appreciate the advantage of tax-free income, consider the following fact: The average American taxpayer spends the first 81 days of each working year paying his or her federal income taxes; this is up from 74 days just 5 years ago. It is not a very appealing thought to think that, on average, each of us spends almost one-fourth of our working lives working for Uncle Sam. The numbers become very disturbing when you include the amount of additional money you shell out each year in the form of sales tax, property tax, and gasoline taxes (there are even more taxes out there, but I think you get the point).

It's What You Keep that Counts

Every April 15th, you lose as much as 38.59% of your investment income. That's up to $386 of federal and California state taxes for every $1,000 you earn. If you do not live in California, the amount going to your state (and city in a few instances) may end up being higher or lower than this figure.

To fully appreciate the combined effect of federal and state income taxes, look at the chart below, which assumes a California taxpayer. As you can see, if you are married and have taxable income between $57,670 and $86,500, you would have to earn 9.19% on a pre-tax basis to equal a 6% tax-free rate of return. A return of 9.19% is certainly possible, but such an investment would entail more risk than owning a 6% municipal bond.

Taxable Income		Combined CA & Fed. Income Tax Bracket	A California tax-exempt yield of the following is equivalent to a fully taxable yield of:		
Joint	Single		5.00%	5.50%	6.00%
$32,870-$35,800	$16,435-$21,450	20.10%	6.26%	6.88%	7.51%
$35,800-$45,632	$21,450-$22,816	32.32%	7.39%	8.13%	8.87%
$45,632-$57,670	$22,816-$28,835	33.76%	7.55%	8.30%	9.06%
$57,670-$86,500	$28,835-$51,900	34.70%	7.66%	8.42%	9.19%
$86,500-$200,000	$51,900-$100,000	37.42%	7.99%	8.79%	9.59%
$200,000-$400,000	$100,000-$200,000	37.90%	8.05%	8.86%	9.66%
$400,000-and up	$200,000-and up	38.59%	8.14%	8.96%	9.77%

Interest paid on tax-free investments is generally lower than interest paid on taxable investments like corporate bonds and bank CDs. But you should compare the yields on tax-free investments to taxable investments only after you have considered the municipal's tax advantage. The result will be the taxable equivalent yield—the yield you'll have to get on a similar taxable investment to equal the tax-free yield.

Municipal bonds are not for investors who are in a low tax bracket. Such investors who want to be in bonds are better off in corporate or government issues. Furthermore, municipals should never be used in a retirement plan. There is only one way to make tax-free income taxable, and that is to put it into an IRA, pension, or profit-sharing plan. Everything that comes out of these plans is fully taxable by the Fed (assuming the contributions were all deductible).

A Simple Formula

If you don't want to use the table on the previous page, you may find the formula below more useful. Thus, to determine if municipal bonds make sense for you, use this formula:

Tax-Free Yield/(1–Client's Tax Rate)=Taxable Equivalent Yield

As an example, suppose you are in the 31% tax bracket and not sure whether you should buy a municipal bond with a yield of 6.25% or a government bond with a yield of 8%. By using the formula above, you can see that the tax-free bond makes much more sense (in this example, the government bond would have to have had a yield of over 9.06% to be a better choice).

6.25%/(1–.31)= 9.06% Taxable Equivalent

Looked at another way, compare how much income you

earn and keep from a $10,000 tax-free investment yielding 6.00% to what you earn and keep from a similar $10,000 taxable investment yielding 7.50%.

	Tax-Free Investment	Taxable Investment
Total income earned	$600	$750
Income lost to taxes	$0	$233
Income you keep	$600	$517

Missed Opportunity

Tax-free investing is gaining popularity, but many investors are still sitting on the sidelines. According to the most recent IRS data available, less than 15% of households with adjusted gross incomes (AGIs) of $75,000 to $100,000 reported tax-exempt income; under 23% of households with AGIs of $100,000 to $200,000 reported tax-exempt income. Unaware of the advantages, or perhaps lacking confidence in their investing know-how, many investors are needlessly losing part of their hard-earned income to taxes.

Taxes can take a heavy toll on your investments: *Federal* income taxes alone can take up to 31% of your earned income. And high state and local taxes increase your tax-bite even more. It is doubtful that tax rates will decline under Clinton, at least not during his first term. It's inevitable that high taxes, combined with declining interest rates, should lead many investors to consider the benefits of tax-free investing. You should consider investing in tax-free securities if you're single, with 1992 taxable income expected to exceed $21,450, or if you file a joint return with income over $35,800.

You can purchase municipal bonds individually or within a unit trust or mutual fund. Individual bonds pay interest every six months and have a set maturity date (although they can be sold at anytime prior to maturity). Mutual funds give you the flexibility of being able to move part or all of your municipal bond fund money into another type of fund (for example, government securities, high-yield bonds, international stocks, and money markets) with a telephone call and at a cost of only five dollars. Funds can also be structured so that interest is sent to you each month, or automatically reinvested into the fund.

Funds and Unit Trusts

A great deal has been written about mutual funds in periodicals and books. Chapter 1, *Money Market Funds*, also gave a definition of a mutual fund. So, not to be repetitious, let us focus our attention on what a unit trust is, how it works, and how it can benefit us as investors.

A unit investment trust (UIT) is a package of securities such as municipal, corporate, or US government bonds. UITs may also invest in government mortgage-backed securities, zero coupon bonds, and equities as well. Unlike mutual funds, which may buy and sell securities at any time, a UIT is not managed. To create a UIT, a professional money manager selects securities from a range of offerings and maturities. Then the UIT is closed and usually no new securities are added for the life of the trust. UITs are available with maturities ranging from one year to 30 years.

Since the portfolio remains relatively unchanged during the life of the trust (except for bonds that are "called away"—prematurely redeemed, by the issuer), you can predict the return from your shares should you hold them to maturity. Depending on the trust you choose, you can receive predictable income on a monthly, quarterly, semi-annual, or annual basis.

While most UITs impose a sales charge, there are no ongoing management fees. However, there are annual fees that are deducted from the yield; such fees are a small fraction of one percent. Any fees will be listed in the trust prospectus.

The portfolio of a UIT is generally divided into $1000 or $100 units. As an investor, you can choose the number of units you would like to purchase. You can sell or redeem any or all of your units at any time. The terms for redemption are set prior to your original purchase. The value you receive for your units is based on current market factors. The redemption price may be higher or lower than the original price paid, depending on market conditions at the time of sale. Any capital gains are subject to federal, state, and local taxes.

While bonds cannot be added to the unit trust after it is closed, the sponsor may receive principal from a bond called prior to maturity, or sell certain securities if circumstances demand. And since the proceeds from the redemption of a bond cannot be reinvested in the trust, they are distributed to investors before the trust matures. Unit trusts may hold from a dozen to 50 or more securities, offering an easy way to diversify an investment. Diversification helps reduce risk. Since a UIT cannot be changed, you cannot automatically reinvest your earnings into the trust itself, unlike a mutual fund.

UIT sponsors typically select securities from the top four grades—AAA to BBB—as rated by Moody's Investor Service or Standard and Poor's Corporation. Some trusts offer insurance on portfolio holdings, which guarantees timely payment of principal and interest. And bonds held within the trust may be insured until maturity. The prospectus of the trust, which you are given prior to or at the time of purchase, provides you with the ratings of the securities in the portfolio and whether insurance is offered.

Track Record

Historical returns over the past three, five, 10, and 15 years for municipal funds are shown following (for periods ending 11/30/92). All of the figures shown in the table below are average *annual* rates of return. As you can see, there is little difference between the taxable returns offered by US government bonds and the tax-free yields of municipal bonds (out of fairness to government bonds, it should be pointed out that these are all total return figures: Yield plus appreciation of principal or minus loss of principal).

	Years			
Category	3	5	10	15
Municipal Bond Funds	8.4%	9.2%	10.4%	7.4%
US Government Bond Funds	8.9%	9.2%	10.2%	9.4%
Rate of Inflation (CPI)	4%	4.2%	3.8%	5.7%

Three Ways to Go

Unit trusts and mutual funds account for over two-thirds of municipal ownership. There are three different categories of municipal bond funds and unit trusts: National, state-free, and high yield.

National municipal bond funds and unit trusts are made of debt instruments issued by a wide range of states. These funds are exempt from federal income taxes only. To determine what small percentage is also exempt from state income taxes, consult the fund's prospectus and look for the weighting of US Territory issues (for example, The Virgin Islands, Guam, Puerto Rico), District of Columbia items, and obligations from your state of residence.

State-free, sometimes referred to as *double tax-free*, funds and unit trusts invest only in bonds and notes issued in a particular state. You must be a legal resident of that state to avoid paying state income taxes on the fund's income (capital gains are still taxable). As an example, most California residents who are in a high tax bracket will only want to consider purchasing a municipal bond fund that has the name "California" in it. Residents of New York who purchase a California tax-free fund will escape federal income taxes, but not state and any local taxes.

High-yield, tax-free funds and unit trusts invest in the same types of issues found in a national municipal bond fund, but with one important difference. By seeking higher returns, high-yield funds look for lower-rated issues and bonds that are not rated. A municipality may not get a rating for its issue because of the costs involved compared to the relatively small size of the bond or note being floated. There are many non-rated issues that are very safe. These types of municipal bond funds are relatively new, but should not be overlooked by the tax conscious investor. High-yield, tax-free funds have demonstrated less volatility and higher return than their other tax-free counterparts.

Less Volatility

Until the early 1980's, municipal bonds were almost as sensitive to interest-rate changes as corporate and government bonds. During the last several years, however, tax-free bonds have taken on a new personality. Now, when interest rates change, municipal bonds exhibit only one-half to one-third the price change that occurs with similar funds made up of corporate or government issues. This decreased volatility is due to a smaller supply of municipal bonds and the elimination of almost all tax shelters. This has increased the popularity of tax-free bonds.

T. Rowe Price

To give you an idea as to the benefits of a investing in a high-yield, tax-free fund, look at the results of the T. Rowe Price Tax-Free, High-Yield Fund.

Year	Total Return
1986	+ 20.4%
1987	+ 0.2
1988	+ 11.2
1989	+ 10.5
1990	+ 7.1
1991	+ 11.7
1992	+ 9.0

As you can see, this fund has not experienced a negative year since its July 1985 inception. Even though these are very good returns for a tax-free fund, this portfolio is considered to have low risk. A recent issue of *Morningstar Mutual Funds* ($395 a year, 800-878-5005), a well-respected mutual fund advisory service, gives this fund its highest rating, five stars.

T. Rowe Price offers a number of other mutual funds, including other tax-free portfolios. For additional information, call (800) 638-5660 or write to:

T. Rowe Price Associates
100 E. Pratt St.
Baltimore, MD 21202

Summary

Treasury Secretary Lloyd M. Bentsen has rarely seen a tax break he didn't like. On the other hand, during his last few years as a US senator, he has been one of the more vocal supporters of deficit reduction and higher savings. Municipal bonds are the perfect fit for such a view or cure. Their tax-free status makes them an alluring means for people to save. The federal deficit can be reduced by reduced funding to the states. Each state will then have to look for ways to raise money. Issuing more municipal bonds will, at least for the short-term, be one of the least painful ways to accomplish this transference of spending by the Fed to the states.

Once you begin looking at your yields and returns on an after-tax basis, you will appreciate municipal bonds. This is an often over-looked investment because of its simplicity. Higher tax brackets for the upper-middle class and wealthy mean that these taxpayers need to reacquaint themselves with one of the few remaining sources whose income is free from income taxes. If you are not sure that municipal bonds are for you, review the chart and formula earlier in this chapter. You may be surprised to learn that tax-free investments make sense for your portfolio.

If you are an experienced investor, or merely an investor who is tired of seeing the value of your bonds drop in value whenever interest rates go up (or even *rumors* that rates *may* increase), then you will appreciate municipal bonds even more. The comparatively limited supply of this asset, versus its strong, ongoing demand, is a stabilizing force during uncertain periods of time in the bond market.

Therefore, when rates either go up or are expected to go up, and the value of your government or corporate bonds drop, rest assured that your municipal bonds will not fall nearly as much in value. Municipal bonds, whether owned individually or within a unit trust or mutual fund, have only one-half to one-third the volatility of government bonds or high-quality corporate bonds with similar maturities. In fact, there are several days, weeks, and months each year when government and high-quality issues drop in value and their municipal counterparts remain unchanged in price.

If you feel that your tax bracket or interest rates are going to go up under Clinton then municipal bonds are for you, particularly if you are scared or confused by other investments such as stocks, real estate, and tax-advantaged investments (most of which will be covered in later chapters).

3

Global Bonds

THE INTERNATIONAL MONETARY FUND (IMF) has said that growth in the industrial world as a whole will be 2% in 1993. The IMF predicts that the American economy will grow by about 3% next year, compared to 1% for Germany, 2.5% for Japan (which is low compared to their post-war growth rate), and 1% for Western Europe. Even though these low figures for 1993 are not good for any one of these countries, they are good for certain types of bonds.

It is commonly known by Wall Street that the bond market reacts positively to bad news (for example, lower than expected growth rates, increased unemployment, and higher taxes). The same is true with bond markets around the world. Therefore, although the US may be the only somewhat shining economy in 1993 and during part of 1994 (meaning that domestic bonds may *drop* in price), there are bond opportunities abroad.

As we all know, interest rates in the US have fallen dramatically, making it increasingly difficult for investors to maintain their levels of income. One way more and more investors are responding to this dilemma is by turning to the growing international bond market and investing in a high-quality, investment grade global mutual fund. This strategy enables investors to benefit from those interest-rate trends around the world that offer the greatest potential returns.

As we climb out of our recession and begin to experience decent economic growth, one might think that the US would be the best place to invest. After all, doesn't economic growth go hand in hand with investment opportunities? Well, the answer is either not necessarily or, in the case of bonds, no. As our economy becomes strong once again and businesses raise money by issuing bonds and consumers borrow more to make purchases, the demand for money increases. As demand increases, so do interest rates. This means that long-term bonds will drop in value. (There is an inverse relationship between bond values and interest rates: Whatever interest rates do, bond prices do the exact opposite.) Fortunately for investors, other countries around the world still have high interest rates.

High interest rates and uncertainty over the future of economic uncertainty means that Europe will not fully come out of its recession until long after the US shows robust growth. Despite a decade of having more work than workers, Japan is faced with unemployment. Our biggest trading partner, Canada continues to have a stagnant economy that began in 1990. It is unlikely that America will pull Europe out of its recession this time, as it did in 1984.

As an investor, you can benefit from this climate by investing in foreign, also known as *international*, bonds.

In order to stimulate their economies, Europe, Japan, and Canada, will all be lowering their interest rates. When foreign rates fall, international bond prices appreciate. Without big cuts in interest rates, the economic downturn in these countries will deepen. Poor or nonexistent growth will also affect US exporters such as Ford, GM, Caterpillar, and Outboard Marine.

Assessing the economic environment to evaluate its effect on interest rates and bond values requires an understanding of two important factors: inflation and supply. During inflationary periods, when there is too much money chasing too few goods, government tightening of the money supply helps create a balance between an economy's cash resources and its available goods. *Money supply* refers to the amount of cash made available for spending, borrowing, or investing. Controlled by the central banks of each nation, it is a primary tool used to manage inflation, interest rates, and economic growth.

A prudent tightening of the money supply can help bring on disinflation—decelerated loan demand, reduced durable goods orders, and falling prices. During disinflationary times, interest rates also fall, strengthening the underlying value of existing bonds. While such factors ultimately contribute to a healthier economy, they also mean lower yields for government bond investors. A trend toward disinflation currently exists in markets around the world. The worldwide growth in money supply is at its lowest level in 20 years.

As the US and other governments implement policies designed to reduce inflation, interest rates are dropping. This disinflation can be disquieting to the individual who specifically invests for high monthly income. In reality, falling interest rates mean higher bond values, and investors seeking long-term growth or high total returns can therefore benefit from declining rates. Inflation, which drives interest rates higher, is the true enemy of bond investors. It diminishes bond values and, in addition, erodes the buying power of the interest income that investors receive. Income-seeking investors need to find economies where inflation is coming under control, yet interest rates are still high enough to provide favorable bond yields.

10-Year Government Bond Yields Around the World

Country	Yield
Finland	14.5%
Sweden	13.3%
Denmark	9.6%
Australia	9.0%
United Kingdom	9.0%
France	8.7%
Canada	8.0%
New Zealand	8.0%
Netherlands	7.9%
Germany	7.6%
United States	6.4%
Japan	4.9%

SOURCE: MORGAN STANLEY CAPITAL INTERNATIONAL PERSPECTIVE 9/30/92

The gradually decreasing yields on US bonds compel the investor who seeks high income to think globally. With over half the world's $12 trillion bond market now found outside of the United States, it is clear that investing in the US bond market alone ignores the opportunities for attractive returns offered by global fixed income investments.

While not all bond markets will peak at the same level, they do tend to follow patterns. Targeting those countries where interest rates are at peak levels and inflation is falling results in higher income and creates significant potential for capital appreciation as rates ultimately decline.

World Bond Market

If you are limiting your bond portfolio to US investments, you are missing out on over half of the world's bond market opportunities. Currently, over 55% of the world's government bonds are issued in countries other than the United States. Investing in global bonds can help position US investors' portfolios to benefit from capital growth opportunities in world bond markets, while capturing income from those bonds.

Although the US leads the world in outstanding debt, other countries and foreign corporations also issue IOUs as a way of financing projects and operations. As high as our debt seems, it is not out of line when compared to our GNP (now called *GDP*, Gross Domestic Product). The ratio of our debt to GDP places us squarely in the middle of the pack when compared to the other members of the group of seven (Germany, Japan, Canada, Italy, UK, France, and the US).

World Bond Market, Ranked in Dollar Terms as of December 31, 1991

North America	
United States	44.5%
Canada	2.6
Europe	
Germany	9.0%
Italy	6.2
France	4.7
United Kingdom	2.7
Belgium	2.1
Sweden	1.9
Denmark	1.6
Switzerland	1.4
Netherlands	1.4
Spain	0.9
Austria	0.6
Norway	0.3
Finland	0.3
Others	1.3
Pacific Basin	
Japan	17.8%
Australia and New Zealand	0.7

Track Record

Over the past 30 calendar years, non-US bonds have provided an average advantage of 2.9 percentage points a year (10.2% vs. 7.3%) compared with US bonds. Here's the record for other periods through December 31, 1991:

Average Annual Compound Return

Time Frame	Non-US Bonds	US Bonds	Additional Yearly Return Provided by Non-US Bonds
5 years	12.5%	9.6%	+2.9%
10 years	14.2	13.7	+0.5
20 years	11.6	9.4	+2.2

Over the past 25 years, international bonds have outperformed US bonds and inflation. They have come close to matching the return of US common stocks. Since 1962, there have been 20 10-year periods (for example, 1960–1969 and 1961–1970). The *Non*-US Bond Index has *outperformed* the US Bond Index in *every* 10-year period since 1962.

Each year since 1984, at least three government bond markets have provided yields higher than those available in the US (Salomon Brothers, Inc.). With almost 50% of the world's bonds found outside the US, investors must look beyond US borders to find bonds offering yields and total returns that meet their investment objectives.

Global bond investors have discovered that superior capital growth opportunities are often found in bond markets outside the United States. In fact, according to J.P. Morgan, over the past five years, while US government bond investors enjoyed an average annual return of 9.4%, the US ranked 10th among global government bond markets.

Historical returns over the past three, five, 10, and 15 years for international (world) bond funds are shown following (for periods ending 11/30/92). All of the figures shown in the table below are average *annual* rates of return.

Category	Years 3	5	10	15
World(global) bond funds	9.9%	8.8%	13.2%	n/a
US Government bond funds	8.9%	9.2%	10.2%	9.4%
Inflation (CPI)	4%	4.2%	3.8%	5.7%

Risk Reduction

Global diversification reduces risk because the major economies around the world do not move up and down at the same time. As we climb out of a recession, Japan may be just entering one, Germany may still be in the middle of one, or both may be true. Similarly, when Italy is trying to stimulate its economy by lowering interest rates, Canada may be raising its rates in order to curtail inflation. By investing in different world bond markets, you are not at the mercy of any one country's political environment or fiscal policy.

The Currency Issue

When you buy international bonds, you are purchasing securities issued in a foreign currency, such as the Japanese yen or the English pound. Prospective investors need to be aware of the potential changes in the value of the foreign currency relative to the US dollar. As an example, if you were to invest in Australian dollar-denominated bonds that had a current yield 15%, and that currency appreciated 12% against the US dollar, your total return for the year would be 27%. Conversely, if the Australian dollar declined by 20% against the US dollar, your total return would be –5%.

Despite this rather extreme example, the currency issue becomes a non-issue when you are looking at performance over a 5–10 year period or longer. This is because the dollar goes up in value (making foreign bonds look less attractive) and the dollar drops in value (making foreign bonds look even better). Over any meaningful period of time, investors' concern over the direction and strength of the US dollar is unwarranted.

Trying to figure out if the dollar will go up or down in value over any given period, whether a day, week, month, or year, is as difficult as trying to guess what interest rates or the stock market will do. The currency issue should only concern you if you expect to hold foreign securities or international mutual funds for only a few years. If this is the case, you may want to invest in a fund that practices currency hedging (which protects foreign security owners *if* the dollar does appreciate).

Keep in mind that if you are wrong, and the dollar does not appreciate against the foreign currencies represented in your portfolio, your return will not be as high as a portfolio or mutual fund that does not practice currency hedging. Since hedging is a form of insurance, there is a price to be paid. The price eats into the returns of funds and unit trusts that use this type of insurance. Most global bond and foreign stock funds do not practice currency hedging extensively. This should give you some good insight into the benefits of such a practice. Obviously, most money managers consider currency hedging to normally be a waste of time.

Credit and Market Risk

Even with high income as the primary goal, investors must consider credit and market risk. By investing primarily in government-guaranteed bonds from the world's most creditworthy nations, you can get an extra measure of credit safety for payment of interest and repayment of principal. By diversifying across multiple markets, fund managers can significantly reduce market risk as well. Diversification is a proven technique for controlling market risk. Since foreign markets do not necessarily move in tandem with US markets, each country represents varying investment opportunities at different times.

The Components of Return

Most investors understand the concept of investing in global bonds for the income, or yield, they provide. However, many investors do not realize that global bonds may offer more than just yield. There are three components to successfully managing global bond portfolios: Capital appreciation, yield, and currency management (described earlier). Investors searching strictly for high yields may lose out on capital appreciation opportunities. By the same token, those looking solely for capital appreciation often give up current income. Finally, individuals who invest in global bonds, without applying the principles of currency management, can see their investment temporarily erode when exchange rates change adversely.

Investing in global bonds provides you with the potential for capital appreciation during periods of declining interest rates. An inverse relationship exists between bond values and interest rates. When interest rates fall, as is the case in most bond markets in the world today, existing bond values climb. Conversely, as interest rates rise, the value of existing bonds declines. For example, if an investor holds a bond paying 9% interest, and interest rates for newly issued bonds climb to 10%, the value of the 9% bond declines. However, if interest rates for newly issued bonds decline to 8%, the bond paying 9% appreciates in value, reflecting the desirability of the higher-yielding bond.

Historically, inflation has been the key factor in driving worldwide interest rates higher. Inflation diminishes bond returns and erodes the buying power of the investor's principal. In the 1990's, a worldwide trend toward disinflation is developing. Our own Federal Reserve has been actively battling inflation, and as a result, has been able to lower key interest rates in an effort to strengthen the US economy. This trend should continue in the US and will spread to other nations such as Germany and Japan throughout the 1990's. Targeting those countries where interest rates are at peak levels *and* inflation is falling not only results in higher income, but also creates significant potential for capital appreciation.

The Benefits of Using Mutual Funds

As you can see, investing overseas is much trickier than buying domestic assets. You should only buy individual foreign bonds if you have the time to become an expert in the economies around the world, tax laws, and treaties in the countries you plan on dealing with. Also, you should be able to spot future trends wherever they may exist. In other words, if you do not view your portfolio as a full-time job, use unit trusts and mutual funds instead.

Global bond funds, particularly those that have a high concentration in foreign issues, are an excellent risk-reduction tool that the vast majority of investors should use. One of the very best fund managers in this area is Van Eck.

Van Eck

The Van Eck Organization has been investing worldwide since their founding in 1955. Their Chairman, John C. Van Eck, was one of the first investment managers in the United States to realize the opportunities available through global diversification of the investment portfolio.

Van Eck is uniquely positioned as a global adviser. Over the past 37 years, the company has established a seasoned team of investment professionals with an average of over 20 years of experience in the global marketplace. Led by a European-trained strategist, they manage global accounts in several currencies for both European and American clients. Van Eck manages accounts with assets totaling over $1.2 billion.

Van Eck specializes in global investment. Their single-mindedness of purpose has allowed them to dedicate 100 percent of their resources to the global sector, an approach that has proven to be successful. As a result, their global fixed-income record has consistently outperformed both the competition and the benchmarks by substantial margins.

The objectives of the World Income Fund (part of the Van Eck family) are almost equally divided between total return and current income. However, they achieved approximately 70% of their total return over the years through income rather than capital appreciation. The average maturity of the bonds in the portfolio is 5 1/2 years; in Europe, a long-term bond has only a 10-year maturity (versus 15–30 years for US bonds). The fund reduces risk by globally diversifying its portfolio of debt securities, based on the fundamental economic strength of a broad range of countries and currencies. The following table shows the track record of the World Income Fund (for periods ending 11/30/92):

Period	Average Annual Return	Total Return
2 years	7.1%	14.7%
3 years	11.1%	37.0%
5 years	11.3%	70.5%
Life of fund	10.8%	77.5%

The political factors Van Eck focuses on include leadership crises, electoral pressures, and the monetary/fiscal policy decisions that stem from these factors. There are economic factors such as trade and current account balances, GNP, productivity, unit-labor costs, money-supply growth, capacity utilization, commodity prices, capital investment, and demographics.

Van Eck also offers other mutual funds, including:

- International Investors (founded in 1955, it is the oldest and largest gold-oriented mutual fund in the US).
- Short-Term World Income Fund (which seeks the highest level of current income with minimal fluctuation by sticking to high-quality debt securities with remaining maturities of not more than three years).
- World Trends Fund (global stocks).
- The US Government Money Fund (a very conservative money market account).

For additional information, call (800) 221-2220, or write to:

Van Eck Securities Corporation
122 East 42ND St.
New York, NY 10168

Summary

Members of the Clinton Administration know that one of the best means of stimulating domestic growth is by increased exports. The way to stimulate US exports is to make spending easier abroad. One of the first places to look is Germany, the economic locomotive of Europe. In recent years, the Bundesbank has had to raise rates to lower an unacceptable (by German standards) inflation rate of 4%. As Germany's inflation rate drops to the 2–3% range, the Bundesbank will be able to lower its interest rates. In the alternative, if the US becomes more fiscally responsible, the German central bank may have the excuse it needs to lower rates.

Lower rates in Germany are necessary for economic stimulation in Europe which, in turn, will benefit the US economy by increased export demand. If short-term rates remain high in Germany, other countries will be forced to keep their rates *even higher* to make sure that money does not pour into German debt instruments.

As an investor, you will also need to watch what Japan does. There is little leeway for the Japanese to lower their rates any further. Instead, you should be looking at how huge Japan's promised public-works program will be—a signal to higher growth. Nevertheless, both of these economic superpowers will be closely watching what goes on in Washington. Any type of serious deficit-reduction package will almost certainly be met with rate cuts in both of these countries. A drop in rates will translate into greater spending, which, in turn, will benefit us at home.

Global, foreign, and international bonds offer you an excellent opportunity to participate in some healthy appreciation as interest rates fall overseas. You may have missed a similar opportunity when rates were falling in the US, but you are not too late if you look outside our borders.

Besides offering higher yields than their US counterparts, foreign bonds, when added to a portfolio of domestic securities and real estate, actually reduce your overall level of risk. This is an area that has been largely overlooked by the majority of Americans; hopefully, you will not overlook them.

4

High-Yield Bonds

The financial services industry overwhelmingly supported the reelection of George Bush because they were afraid that a Democratic president would raise interest rates. The Republican Party tried, unsuccessfully, to convince the electorate that President Bush was actually running against Jimmy Carter, a president blamed for high interest rates and inflation during the late 1970's. Surprisingly, the financial press did an about-face soon after the election and before the inauguration. There is now a strong consensus in the financial community that rates will stay low during at least the next few years, despite an initial increase in the deficit.

In light of a low-interest rate environment, investors are looking at alternatives for their maturing CDs and government securities. Most of the options do not seem to really stand out from the crowd, except for two: international bonds (detailed in the previous chapter) and high-yield bonds.

As Clinton's proposals are put into place and the economy strengthens, the US dollar may strengthen due to a rise in US interest rates (as bond yields increase, so does their attractiveness to foreign investors) or some type of meaningful deficit-reduction program (more likely in 1995–96). If this happens, you will need to reassess any foreign securities holdings you might have, whether in individual international bonds, global equities, or mutual funds and unit trusts that invest in foreign securities. A strong dollar is bad for US investors who own overseas assets (for example, if the dollar increases 3% against country x, the securities of that country will decline on paper by exactly 3% unless there is some type of rally in x's markets).

If you start to see the US dollar strengthen, then you should do one of two things:

1. Limit your foreign holdings to countries whose currencies are tied to the dollar (for example, virtually anywhere in the Pacific Basin except Japan and Australia).
2. Look at domestic securities, such as high-yield bonds, as an alternative or addition to your portfolio.

Before detailing the pros and cons of high-yield bonds, let us first do a quick review as to how bonds work.

Bonds are issued by corporations to raise money. If the issuing corporations were more financially secure, had been around longer, or both, they would issue *investment-grade*, also known as *bank-quality* securities. Since the great majority of corporations in America do not have the financial clout to issue AAA, AA, A, or BAA rated bonds, they are forced to issue "junk." Investors are attracted to high-yield bonds because of their better-than-average rate of return.

Virtually any corporation can issue bonds. The public decides if it is going to buy these bonds. There are major rating services that evaluate the current and projected financial stability of these companies. Ratings range from AAA down to D (for "in default"). Some bonds are not rated because the issuing corporation or municipality was not willing to pay the rating service fee, which can end up costing tens of thousands of dollars.

When the US economy is going through the initial or middle stages of a recession, high-yield bonds may drop in value. This is because there is a perceived, and sometimes real, concern that corporations that are not among the strongest in financial terms, will default or suspend their obligations. During the later stages of a recession, such as early 1991, junk bonds experienced tremendous gains. Some high-yield corporate bond funds were up over 40% for 1991, easily beating out all other types of bond funds and even outperforming several categories of stock funds. As the economy strengthens, investor and consumer confidence increases along with the belief that corporate America will survive. Such assurances translate into additional appreciation for high-yield bonds.

Poorly rated bonds appeal to a much smaller, more aggressive, investor base. Since there is less demand for these securities, the issuing corporations must enhance their yields to attract buyers. The resulting yields, also known as *coupon rates* for junk bonds, are anywhere from two to six percentage points higher than corporate bonds that are considered extremely safe.

The Difference Between Junk and High-Yield Bonds

In reality, there is a big difference between junk and high-yield bonds, even though these terms are frequently used to mean the same thing. *Junk* bonds were those debt instruments used for corporate takeovers (trying to buy another company with paper instead of sweat, hard work, and cash). *High-yield* bonds really represent those securities that have had a long track record of overall reliability for the timely payment of interest and principal; they also represent those bonds that have had comparatively few defaults.

The Realities of Risk

According to Salomon Brothers, junk bond defaults averaged only 0.84% from 1980 to 1984. This rate almost tripled from 1985 to 1989 as defaults averaged 2.24% per year. Then, in 1990, defaults surged to 4.6%. Junk bonds rated BB performed closer to high-quality bonds than lower-rated junk issues. For example, during 1990, BB-rated bonds declined only slightly in price and actually delivered positive returns (once the current yield was factored in). Bonds rated CCC declined over 30% in price. Well over 90% of the junk bonds in existence at the end of 1989 were issued since 1982.

Track Record

You may be surprised to learn that during most periods of time, junk bonds have outperformed high quality corporate, municipal, and US government securities. Their return has been better on a current yield, or return, basis and on a *total return* basis (current income plus appreciation or minus depreciation). Even for the past 10 years ending 1991 or 1992, junk bonds had better returns, despite the beating they took during 1989 and 1990. You may remember this time as "merger mania" or "leveraged buyouts;" a period when it seems that individual and institutional investors were buying junk bonds no matter how shaky they were. Let us examine in greater detail what happened during the later part of 1989 and during 1990.

First there was adverse legislation. In the summer of 1989, Congress essentially outlawed the savings and loan industry from investing in the high-yield market. This placed the S & L industry, then holder of 11% of all outstanding high-yield securities, under tremendous selling pressure. Second, there was regulation. The National Association of Insurance Commissioners, the regulatory body of the life insurance industry, tightened quality requirements for life insurance portfolios and restricted the use of high-yield credits. That forced life insurers, who then owned 30% of all outstanding high-yield bonds, to step back from such a market. Third, there was negative publicity. Press reports on the bankruptcy of Drexel-Burnham-Lambert, the largest underwriter of high-yield bonds, in February 1990 shock consumer confidence and spurred large cash outflows by mutual fund companies. Finally, there was the Persian Gulf War. When Iraq invaded Kuwait in August 1990 the financial markets started discounting the beginning of a recession in the US economy.

When measured by *total return*, there certainly have been periods of time when safer securities performed much better than their high-yield brethren. This is particularly true when you look at certain one-, three-, and five-year periods. Yet, over most of these same time horizons, and particularly when you look at 10 or more year periods of time, junk bonds are normally the winner when compared to other US bonds.

To see how these bonds have fared over shorter periods of time, let us look at all of the five-year periods beginning with 1982 (the figures are based on the Lipper

High-Yield Universe Average, an index of high-yield bond funds compiled and tracked by a neutral advisory source). The figures that follow are total return numbers, they are not annualized.

1982–1986	+121.1%
1983–1987	+ 75.4%
1984–1988	+ 69.1%
1985–1989	+ 52.3%
1986–1990	+ 11.1%
1987–1991	+ 36.5%
1988–1992	+ 77.4%

Historical returns over the past three, five, 10, and 15 years for corporate bond funds are shown as follows (for periods ending 12/31/92). All of the figures shown in the table below are average *annual* rates of return.

	Years			
Category	**3**	**5**	**10**	**15**
High Yield Bond Funds	12.6%	9.4%	10.1%	10.5%
Corporate Bond Funds (High Quality)	9.4%	9.5%	10.6%	9.7%
Inflation (CPI)	4%	4.2%	3.8%	5.7%

Reduced Volatility

As you might suspect, the biggest risk with high-yield bonds is the risk of default. No one likes to own a bond that has stopped or suspended paying interest. More importantly, no one likes to have their principal in jeopardy of not being paid back. As mentioned earlier, even the number of junk bonds that default is very small compared to the thousands that perform just fine. Losses from defaults are rarely 100 cents on the dollar. At least one study shows that investors get back approximately 70 cents on the dollar when this worst-case situation occurs.

Although high-yield bonds may exhibit greater volatility than their investment-grade peers, they are safer when it comes to *interest rate* risk. Since junk issues have high-yielding coupons and shorter maturities than quality corporate bond funds, they fluctuate less in value when interest rates change. Thus, during periods of expansion in the economy, when interest rates are rising, high-yield funds will generally drop less in value than high-quality corporate or government bond funds. Conversely, when interest rates are falling, government and corporate bonds will appreciate more in value than junk funds.

High-yield bonds resemble equities at least as much as they do traditional bonds in terms of economic cycles and important technical factors. Studies show that only 19% of the average junk fund's total return is explained by the up or down movement of the Lehman Brothers Government/Corporate Bond Index (which measures the performance of bonds in general). To give an idea of how low this number is: 94% of a typical *high-quality* corporate bond fund's performance is explainable by movement in the same index. Indeed, even international bond funds have a higher correlation coefficient than junk, 25% of their performance is explained by the index.

High-Yield Bond Funds

In the case of high-yield bond funds, there is a wide range of current income, quality, and total return. Just as you cannot condemn the entire stock market because some stocks went down last week or last year, you cannot paint the entire high-yield bond market with the single stroke of a brush. The world of bonds is not black and white; it cannot be compartmentalized with a simple description such as "investment grade" or "junk." There are several shades of gray, and it is important that you understand the distinctions, for some of these shades can provide you with some handsome returns.

Only one or two percent of the outstanding corporate bond market experience such troubles each year. Equally important, those that do often are able to turn themselves around and show a profit as well as pay off all bondholders.

High-yield bond funds contain issues that range in quality from BBB to C; a rating less than single-C means that the bond is in default, and payment of interest, principal, or both are in arrears. High-yield bond funds perform best during good economic times. Traditional investors should avoid such issues during periods of recession, since the underlying corporations may have difficulty making interest and principal payments when business slows down. However, these bonds, like common stocks, can perform very well during the second half of a recession. As an example, our most recent recession began in July 1990 and ended in March 1991. High-yield bonds were up over 36% during 1991.

When it comes to high-yield bonds, investors would be wise to accept a lower yield in return for more stability of principal and appreciation potential. This means looking at bonds with a BB or B rating, versus issues rated CCC or lower. A company that has always been concerned with quality and reducing the risk of its investors is Phoenix.

The Phoenix Family of Funds

Phoenix is one of the few fund families that performs well across the board. Their growth, aggressive growth, balanced, and convertible securities funds are all quite impressive. Often, rating services and financial writers do not adequately address the issue of risk. Investors would avoid a great number of mutual funds and other investments if they knew what kind of risk was being incurred. Phoenix, on the other hand, has been able to turn in top returns with comparatively low risk. Their results change from impressive to outstanding once such performance figures are *risk-adjusted.*

The Phoenix High-Yield Bond Fund is no exception. Look at the kind of returns this fund has enjoyed while exposing its investors to minimal risk—a difficult feat for the majority of high-yield or junk-bond funds.

Year	Total Return
1981	+ 8%
1982	+ 30.3
1983	+ 13.4
1984	+ 7.9
1985	+ 21.1
1986	+ 15.9
1987	+ 1.7
1988	+ 13.6
1989	− 1
1990	+ 24.7
1991	+ 24.7
1992	+ 17

What is particularly impressive about this fund is that it has only had one negative year since its July 1980 inception. This is nothing short of amazing when you consider what a beating some high-yield bonds took in 1989 and during the first half of 1990.

For additional information, call (800) 243-4361 or write to:

Phoenix Equity Planning
100 Bright Meadow Blvd.
PO Box 2200
Enfield, CT 06083

Summary

President Clinton has a fine line to walk: Economic stimulation without raising rates. If long-term rates go up because of the bond market's perception of too large a deficit increase, the core of our recovery, the housing industry, will suffer. It will also be more costly for corporate America to do business (servicing a company's debt can eat a large percentage of a company's revenues). If tax rates for corporations and individuals go up too much, corporations will hire fewer people, and the populace will have fewer dollars to spend.

Even those people who did not vote for Bill Clinton acknowledge that he is one of the brightest and politically adept politicians that ever occupied the Oval Office. If anyone can walk this delicate path, it is he. As an investor, you can earn extra money by buying high quality, high yield corporate bonds and, at the same time, watch the security of your investment increase as the economy grows by whatever means.

While government and investment grade bonds may end up showing nominal *or negative* returns during the next few years, high-yield issues would show the best returns.

5

Markets Around The World

ONE OF THE KEYS to successful investing is buying assets that are still somewhat hidden treasures. A great deal of attention has been focused on how US stocks have performed, as measured by the Dow. Headlines are filled with stories about IBM, Ford, GM, and other corporate giants. What has been given little attention are the small and medium-sized corporations that are truly the backbone of this country.

President Clinton understands the importance of the entrepreneurial spirit as it relates to job growth and increased tax revenues. It will be these small companies (those with a net worth of a billion dollars or less) that will kick-start the economy, giving confidence to larger companies and the consumer.

The stocks of big companies will fare well, but such appreciation will come *after* the small-stock sector has taken off. Foreign stocks, detailed in two chapters, should also outperform Dow stocks during the next few years, but for slightly different reasons.

Let us first look at the difference between the different domestic stock markets and then move to a comparison between US and foreign equities. This chapter will lay some important groundwork for the two chapters that follow.

Blue chip stocks, such as those found in the Dow Jones Industrial Average (DJIA) and the Standard & Poor's 500 (S & P 500) have performed similarly under both Democratic and Republican administrations. Over the past half century, the annual returns for these "large cap" stocks has been about 12% compounded. Small cap stocks, those corporations that have outstanding stock worth $1 billion or less, have actually *dropped* close to 2% per year under Republicans. These same issues have grown at close to 17% per year under Democrats.

You should be careful about how you invest in the general market during the next year. Over the past 20 years, the Dow has had an average volatility of 28%; in 1991 it was 7.6%. Since the 1920's, there have only been a few times when there were two years of low volatility back to back. However, do not be over alarmed; volatility can be upward as well as downward. Nevertheless, it is suggested that you stay away from most large domestic stocks for the following reasons:

1. Clinton will increase their costs of doing business by indexing the minimum wage.
2. Passage of the 12-week family leave bill.
3. New legislation will make it illegal to replace striking workers.
4. Other legislation that will ease the Federal burden and increase the costs of doing business for big companies but will exempt small businesses.

Expectations

Here is what you should expect for US stocks under Clinton:

1. The market should peak during the first half of 1993. We have been in a bull market since 1974, with only a few brief interruptions: 1982 and part of 1987.
2. Presidents do unpopular things in their first two years; usually the biggest market gains have come during the *last two years* of their first term.
3. The market is close to historic highs, price/earnings ratios are also very high; the blue chips are either fairly priced or overvalued. The best bet is small cap stocks and capital goods stocks, both large and small (for example, machinery companies, computer companies, technology companies, semi-conductor companies, and telecommunications).
4. There should be a rally during the first few months of 1993 because institutional cash reached its highest level for the year in August 1992, a good number of stocks have had significant corrections, and there is a feeling of hope versus the general down mood for several months prior to the election.
5. Socially responsible companies should be a good investment (highly favored by Vice President Gore).
6. In general, the young growing companies are still a good place to be (they can react more quickly to change and will be exempted from much of the adverse legislation that is likely to pass).

To get bargains, you have to buy at the point of maximum pessimism. The public certainly does not do this and most professionals do not do this either. It is difficult to do because it is much more comfortable to buy when everyone else is buying. However, if you are going to produce superior results, you must not buy when (and what) everyone else is buying. Look for the nation and industries where investors are the most pessimistic, and buy when people are most pessimistic.

Our current low-interest rate and low-inflation environment are favorable to equity prices over the long run. The main cause of low interest rates is excess cash and this also helps fuel stocks. However, over the next generation or so, expect the average increase in the cost of living to be approximately six percent annually.

The stock market is the most advanced and reliable of all leading indicators. Big money goes to the wise people in most cases and this is why the market has been going up recently despite the pessimism. The smart, experienced investors who deal with huge money have the capability to look ahead and know what to expect. That is why the stock market is such a reliable leading indicator. Journalists and the media are the best *lagging* indicator.

Journalists and the media emphasize the negative even after the fact. For example, it seems we have to be a full year into a recovery before the media acknowledges that there is a recovery. The recession ended in May of 1991, but it was not until December 1992 that this was reported. This is why it is important to remember that by the time you read it in the paper it is too late. It is critical to try to overcome human nature as most investors buy when their neighbors are bragging about their gains, but this is actually the time to be taking profits; you should be buying when your friends are selling out of panic.

Health Care

Clinton's two biggest concerns for health care are greater access and cost containment, both of which present significant opportunities for a host of entrepreneurial health-care companies. Developing industries like home care, long-term and rehabilitation care, outpatient surgery and other service businesses stand to gain from nearly any of the reform scenarios.

While health care is near the top of Clinton's agenda, the President's penchant for consensus building should ensure that major health-care reform measures will evolve over the next four years. Congress, it will be remembered, learned a hard lesson a few years ago when it enacted and then repealed Medicare catastrophic-care legislation before selling the public on the idea.

There's no shortage of statistical evidence supporting the need for health-care reform. Medical-care expenditures, which currently total roughly 13% of gross domestic product, will grow to 18% of output by the year 2000 if current trends continue. Health-care outlays are growing at more than 10% a year.

While health-care expenditures have been rising, who's paying has changed. Out-of-pocket payments now total less than 25% of national health expenditures, down from 60% barely 30 years ago. The difference has been made up by third-party payers: Private health insurance and government medical programs.

But despite the increasing number of individuals covered by employer-paid health plans, the percentage of the population that lives without health insurance rose in the past decade, to 14% from 12%, after previously declining for more than 20 years. Currently, roughly 35 million Americans lack health insurance.

The segment that stands to benefit most obviously from cost-containment measures is "managed care," by which Wall Street usually means health maintenance organizations (HMOs). HMOs, which currently enroll more than 39 million Americans, have gained favor because of their wholesale buying power, their ability to restrict a patient's choice of physicians and, as a result, the general curtailment or elimination of unnecessary medical procedures.

As the managed-care industry receives increased focus as a potential source of health care for currently uninsured people, it's likely that HMO companies will seek to expand their geographic presence or their array of services. Large HMO operators might stand a better chance of capturing government and private medical-care contracts by adding to the fold smaller companies that focus, for example, on infusion therapy or care for specialty medical conditions.

Small managed-care companies will continue to do well as long as they are in niches that aren't otherwise covered or in their own geographic areas. And they make likely acquisition targets. Alternate-site care companies, including those practicing home infusion care, have also enjoyed a high profile within the medical industry. Home infusion is the practice of providing intravenous drug therapy for patients outside a hospital setting.

A natural progression from home health care is the growing market for patients with long-term illness or debilitation. Long-term care is typically thought of as the nursing-home business, but it's expanding far beyond those boundaries. Because of the growing aged population, long-term care investment opportunities will continue to flourish at least if inflation remains low, a requirement in such a labor-intensive business.

While critics point to physicians fees and high-tech medical devices as the causes of spiraling health-care costs, a low-tech villain is as big a problem: Overhead, which accounts for as much as 18% of the industry's costs. Much of that stems from information-flow requirements, including insurance forms, health-care charts, and the like. One of the hopes among health-care reformers is that those expenses can be cut and the money reallocated for the provision of care.

Besides cost containment and expanded access, President Clinton has identified another area of medical care that's likely to benefit from his tenure and that is high-technology companies. The primary problem faced by potential biotech investors today is that so many companies have only one viable product. If that project gets off track, it could mean death for the company. Mergers are the natural way to enhance the industry's strength and reliability. The US doesn't need 130 publicly traded biotech companies.

The US and Its Trading Partners

Much has been made and will be made of the trade agreements with Mexico and Canada. The elimination of barriers to trade and commerce between Canada, Mexico, and the United States and, ultimately, associated members in Latin America could create demand for US products beyond even the most optimistic expectations.

As for Europe, its governments are already in the process of allowing the markets to dictate equilibrium among and between currencies. When this process is over—the timing is uncertain—interest rates in Europe will decline. These events will result in a revival in European economies and increasing demand for foreign goods that ultimately should translate into renewed vigor in US exports.

We are in one of the most significant interest-rate declines of the postwar period. US rates today, near a 14-year low, are still extraordinarily high, considering inflation. Our inflation was only 2.9% this year, its lowest level since 1976. And with Communism dead, you now have greater than 50% more people in the industrialized world's labor market, and they are willing to work not for $10 an hour but for $1 an hour. So interest rates will be driven lower worldwide.

According to a November 1992 issue of *Business Week*, the folks who run $7 billion worth of institutional investment portfolios do not plan on changing their behavior significantly, despite a new administration. In fact, 74% have stated that a Clinton presidency will have no effect on their near-term global allocation of assets. Only 14% are expected to reduce exposure in US markets.

The Democrat's position over the last few years has not been to oppose a capital gains tax cut outright, but to insist that it be matched with higher taxes on the rich. No capital gains tax cut was enacted because the Republicans refused to pay that price. With income tax rates set to rise, the conditions exist for some kind of capital-gains tax cut.

These changes in individual income taxation could have important portfolio effects. Higher personnel income-tax rates will encourage upper-bracket investors to shift into tax-exempt bonds, a move that has already begun. Stocks with high yields may also be discouraged by the higher rates, especially if a more broad-based capital-gains tax cut is enacted, which would create incentives to shift into growth stocks.

How the Dow has Fared in the First Year

President	Year	Dow
Kennedy	1961	+18.7%
Johnson	1965	+10.9%
Nixon	1969	– 15.2%
Nixon	1973	–16.6%
Carter	1977	– 17.3%
Reagan	1981	– 9.2%
Reagan	1985	+27.7%
Bush	1989	+27.0%

The Foreign Markets

Advances in technology and telecommunications have compressed time, space, and accelerated change. Corporations have pushed into new markets. The economies of nations have become more interrelated and interdependent.

Today, we are on the threshold of a truly global economy. US companies are making light bulbs in Hungary, computers in France, and chemicals in Latin America. Japanese companies are manufacturing cars in Kentucky and Ohio. European conglomerates are marketing biscuits in Boston.

The changes are everywhere. In western Europe, the 12 members that make up the European Community—Belgium, Denmark, France, Greece, Ireland, Italy, Luxembourg, the Netherlands, Portugal, Spain, the United Kingdom, and Germany—have been working to eliminate trade barriers and create the world's largest single free market with more than 300 million consumers. The goal: To permit people and products to move from the Netherlands to Spain as easily as they can from Montana to Florida.

The former Soviet republics and eastern European countries are forging new capitalist economies from the ground up. China, with its 1.2 billion people, is embracing free-market reforms, particularly in its southern coastal provinces. In Latin America, countries have been privatizing state-run industries and opening doors to foreign trade and investment. Canada, the US, and Mexico have created a free-trade zone in North America. In Southeast Asia, governments have endorsed the concept of a regional free-trade area of their own.

Over the past two decades the world's economies have expanded at widely varying rates. The following table sums up the progress from 1972 through 1991. As you can see, some of the biggest gains were recorded by newly industrialized countries such as Taiwan, Singapore, and South Korea. Their growth, even in the face of the current worldwide economic slowdown, continues to be dynamic. More mature economies, such as the United States, grew less but, of course, started from a much higher base.

Worldwide Economic Growth from 1972-1991 (Change in GDP)

Country	Percent Change
Australia	69%
Belgium	52
Brazil	108
Canada	86
China(PRC)	264
France	63
Germany	55
Hong Kong	294
Italy	113
Japan	101
Malaysia	227
Netherlands	48
Philippines	88
Singapore	294
South Korea	404
Spain	75
Sweden	41
Switzerland	30
Taiwan	347
Thailand	271
United Kingdom	47
US	58

SOURCE: INTERNATIONAL MONETARY FUND

In this milieu, global investing has come of age. Twenty years ago, US stocks accounted for about 60% of the world's stock market opportunities, as measured by stock market capitalization. Today that ratio is reversed: It is non-US stocks that account for 60% of the world's market capitalization.

For investors with the flexibility to invest globally, that has meant more choices and opportunities. What's more, non-US stocks have historically produced far superior returns, and they have provided US investors with an opportunity to reduce risk as well. Because the economies of countries around the world often move at different rhythms, declines in some markets are often offset by advances in others, providing an opportunity for greater stability for investors who pursue a multimarket approach.

Given the apparent advantages—flexibility, choice, and opportunity for superior returns with decreased risk—it is little wonder that money in ever-larger accounts flows across national borders in search of attractive investments. Yet the trend toward global investing, while firmly in place, is still in its infancy. Estimates are that in the US, individuals have less than 5% of their investment portfolios in non-US equities. Institutional investors in the US have less than 10% of their assets in stocks of companies with headquarters abroad. Those percentages are widely expected to climb in the years to come.

International Investing: The 25-Year Record

Markets outside the US as a whole have done better than the US market in 16 of the past 25 calendar years. In each of those 16 years, the Morgan Stanley Capital International EAFE index (which reflects all major stock markets outside of North America) has gone up more or declined less than its USA index, which tracks only the US market.

Look at the following table. The figures show how the two averages fared that year. Over the entire 25-year period, the EAFE index gained 1,175%, while the USA index rose 360%. As you can see, in 1989, 1990, and 1991, the US market did better than markets outside the US as a group (1992 made it four years in a row)—the first time this has happened for four consecutive years in more than a quarter-century (the S & P was up 8.4% in 1992 versus –12.2% for the EAFE). Consequently, we are at a point where non-US stocks offer attractive investment opportunities.

1967	1968	1969	1970	1971
+23%	*+28%*	*+3%*	**+1%**	*+26%*
+12%	**+10%**	**–13%**	*–14%*	**+10%**
1972	1973	1974	1975	1976
+33%	*–17%*	*–26%*	*+31%*	**+19%**
+13%	**–19%**	**–31%**	**+30%**	*0%*
1977	1978	1979	1980	1981
+15%	*+29%*	**+8%**	**+23%**	*–5%*
–12%	**0%**	*+2%*	*+19%*	**–9%**
1982	1983	1984	1985	1986
+15%	*+21%*	*+5%*	*+53%*	*+67%*
–5%	**+17%**	**+1%**	**+27%**	**+13%**
1987	1988	1989	1990	1991
+23%	*+27%*	**+27%**	**–6%**	**+27%**
+1%	**+12%**	*+9%*	*–25%*	*+10%*

Note: These expressed in percentages based on US dollars, are for calendar years and do not reflect dividends.

Italic type=all major stock markets outside of North America

Boldface type=US stock market

The Importance of Diversification

One of the themes brought up in this book is the benefit of using mutual funds or unit trusts. The chief reason why these vehicles are recommended is because they offer you instant diversification.

Diversification is the cornerstone of reducing risk, having large holdings of just one stock can be suicide. New York Central Railroad securities were once considered among the safest of all possible investments, but the giant firm eventually collapsed in 1970 despite huge property holdings. Other well-known companies filing for bankruptcy in the last two years include Pan Am World Airways, Macy's, Heileman Brewing, US Home, National Gypsum, Colt Manufacturing, and Southland (Seven-Eleven Stores). At one time, all these companies were considered leaders in their industries.

Even shares of excellent companies can go through lengthy dry spells with little or no return for stockholders. Issues showing zero-net, long-term appreciation for substantial periods include:

DuPont	30 years	1955–1985
Walt Disney	13 years	1972–1985
Gillette	23 years	1961–1984
Coca Cola	13 years	1972–1985
Scott Paper	25 years	1961–1986
McDonald's	10 years	1972–1982
AT&T	20 years	1963–1983
Alcoa	27 years	1965–1983
Campbell Soup	21 years	1961–1982
Hershey Foods	21 years	1961–1982

Even worse, consider the plight of a retiree from one of these firms with a large nest egg tied up in company shares; even with the stock market at an all-time record high these stocks are still lagging badly:

Occidental Petroleum	–68% from 24 years ago
Avon Products	–54% from 19 years ago
General Motors	–45% from 27 years ago
Polaroid	–78% from 23 years ago
Litton Industries	–44% from 33 years ago
Bethlehem Steel	–74% from 33 years ago
Navistar	–96% from 26 years ago

The stock market *as a whole* seems to do well no matter who is president. It is one of those few investments that just keeps going up. In fact, it is the only investment that has consistently and historically outpaced inflation. Before getting into small cap stocks (the next chapter), let us review the stock market in general. First, see what we have to look forward to as economic recovery begins to take hold in the US:

S & P 500 Performance

Recession Begins	1 Year After Recession Begins	2 Years After Recession Begins-Recovery
Nov. 1948	+17.2%	+31.4%
Jul. 1953	+31.9	+47.4
Aug. 1957	+ 9.9	+28.9
Apr. 1960	+24.2	+ 2.9
Dec. 1969	+ 4.0	+14.3
Nov. 1973	–23.8	+36.1
Jan. 1980	+19.3	– 2.2
Jul. 1981	– 13.4	+59.4
Oct. 1990	+27.3	+41.3
Average	**+10.7%**	**+28.8%**

Let us now turn to small cap stocks; one of the few types of US stocks that are expected to do well for the next two years.

6

Small Cap Stocks

As Clinton and Congress find ways to ease the federal burden by reducing spending on a national level, and thereby passing on the costs to the states and private sector, the resulting legislation will hurt some businesses and thereby enhance the competitiveness of others. More specifically, much of big business will suffer due to increased costs of doing business. Smaller companies will be able to escape the new federal requirements, narrowing the economies of scale-of-production costs between themselves and the giants.

It is no secret that some type of national health care plan will be passed during the next couple of years. It is also no surprise that businesses will either pass on such costs to their employees or be forced to shoulder this tremendous burden (for example, automakers have learned that close to $1,000 of the cost of manufacturing a car goes towards paying the health-care costs of its workers). Shifting programs and their costs from the federal to the private sector will not end with health care. And, in some cases, it will be the employee who is shouldered with the burden.

In the past, most retirement plans had the backing, or insurance, of a national pension guarantee fund. This meant that if a corporation did not adequately fund an employee's pension plan, the federal government would step in and make up the difference (up to a certain dollar limit). Such guarantees backed defined benefit plans only (these types of plans assured the employee of a specific monthly dollar benefit at retirement—an amount that was assured long before one's retirement age. Most corporations now have defined *contribution* plans in place. Under these types of plans, an employee's monthly retirement benefit is not guaranteed; the benefits are determined by how well the money has been invested. There is no government-backing if the portfolio underperforms and the retiree ends up with a much smaller pension than expected. The widespread use of these plans minimizes a corporation's financial responsibility and certainly lessens payments from the federal pension guarantee fund.

Health-care legislation, renewed retirement plan requirements, safety requirements, and sick-leave benefits will certainly cover all large businesses, but small companies, through exemptions, will be able to avoid most of these added costs and requirements. So, as the costs of doing business increase for some companies, it will remain relatively level for others. The cost disparities between large and small companies will decrease. Small companies will therefore, almost by default, be able to be more competitive. These firms will also be able to adjust to changes more rapidly, making them better positioned for expansion.

This does not mean that as an investor you cannot benefit by owning common stocks of the larger corporations; it does mean that you must be selective and patient. Look to those blue chip companies that are successfully able to share some of the new financial burdens with its employees, or are able to farm out production to small independents or to foreign subsidiaries, affiliates, and subcontractors. An alternative course of action would be to focus on those businesses that are the least labor intensive.

The bill is coming due for past and present corporate obligations in the areas of health care and retirement benefits, and you do not want to be a shareholder when the tab is presented. However, you will want to jump in once the bad press is out and the stock has dropped accordingly.

If all this sounds too cruel or ghoulish, concentrate on small cap stocks. You won't look like a vulture and you will still be benefiting the economy, employees, and your own pocketbook.

There is no universally agreed-upon definition of what a *small cap stock* is, but the general consensus describes such a security as a *company's stock whose total market capitalization is less than one billion dollars.* Now, a billion dollars may not seem like a small amount to either you or me, but it is considered tiny in the world of financial instruments. Stocks that comprise the Standard & Poor's 500 (S & P 500) have an average market capitalization of $13.7 billion. The stocks that make up the Dow Jones Industrial Average (DJIA) have an even greater average individual market worth. The term *capitalization* simply refers to a company's size—the value of the shares of stock that are outstanding.

Small cap companies differ from larger companies in four fundamental ways:

1. Small cap companies often have more specialized products and market niches.
2. Small cap companies are typically in a different stage of development.
3. Small cap company management often has different characteristics.

4. Small cap firms usually derive most of their income from domestic sales.

Unlike larger companies, which may own a number of smaller operations within different industries, small cap companies focus on innovation. Typically, they will seek to provide one innovative service, product, or technology. While this focus may result in less diversification, it also means that the company's full energies are directed toward succeeding within that one market.

Unlike larger companies, whose products and services are already established, small cap companies are just emerging. In other words, they are at an earlier stage within the corporate life cycle. While this relative youth means uncertainty as to the company's future and chances for long-term success, it also means the company has the opportunity to expand dramatically.

Small cap companies generally have a simpler management structure. Often, a handful of executives will make key decisions. At a larger company, the decision-making process is often slowed because of the number of key management personnel. While the ability to take action quickly is one of the main advantages of small cap companies, it also intensifies the importance of the vision, focus, and execution of their management team.

Often, small cap company success is affected by factors such as:

- **Market share.** How much of the market has this company captured? What are the company's expectations for growth?
- **Opportunities.** What are industry forecasts for this product or service? Does the company have a variety of end users, or is the company dependent on one or two customers only?

- **Recurring revenues.** Can the company count on predictable, long-term income from a reliable source?
- **Plans.** Are the company's plans and expectations realistic? In order to expand, will they be forced to acquire other companies?
- **Control over destiny.** Is the company a strong player in its niche, or is its fate dependent on an outside, controlling concern?

Small Cap Stock Trading

The majority of small cap stocks are traded over-the-counter (OTC), most often through the NASDAQ (National Association of Securities Dealers Automated Quotations). The OTC is not a formal exchange such as the NYSE or AMEX; instead it is comprised of dealers from across the country. Several thousand different OTC stocks are linked together by NASDAQ, a system that allows stockbrokers, financial planners, and anyone with a computer, some inexpensive software and modem, to track these issues by the minute just like stocks listed on an organized exchange such as the NYSE, AMEX, Boston, or Pacific markets.

The most actively traded issues are listed daily in *The Wall Street Journal.* NASDAQ is much bigger than the New York Stock Exchange, which tends to trade larger, more established companies.

Small cap stocks have been around since equities first traded in this country, over 200 years ago. These types of stocks have an excellent, but rocky, track record. Looking at more recent periods of time, for example, small cap stock prices skyrocketed from the mid 1970's to the early 1980's. As blue chip issues became popular in the third quarter of 1982, so did small caps. However, unlike blue chips that had a steady rise of several hundred percentage points from 1982 to October 19, 1987, small cap issues stopped their spectacular gains in 1984.

Returns were modest to mixed for this sector of the market until 1990. During 1990, the average small cap stock dropped close to 22%. In 1991 they did a turnaround, posting gains that averaged close to 60%. The first half of 1992 saw these same stocks drop again, by 15–30% in many cases. Small cap stocks staged another comeback during the second part of 1992, erasing the losses sustained in the first half of the year and then moving to new highs (+12.9% for the 1992 calendar year). The enthusiasm in the second part of 1992 was due to bargain-buying, and the expectation that an accelerated economy under President Clinton will benefit this part of the market in particular.

In making their case for small stocks, enthusiasts aren't deterred by the long dry spell that plagued the shares of smaller companies from mid-1983 to late 1990.

For starters, small stocks normally sparkle during economic recoveries. Following the end of the past seven recessions, small stocks outpaced larger companies' shares for at least 12 months. A major reason: Unlike large multinational corporations, small companies typically make only one or two products, which they sell almost exclusively to US buyers. That narrow focus has meant big trouble for small companies in the current economic slump, but it also should mean fat earnings gains as the US economy picks up steam.

Since mid-1983, the S & P 500 has returned 14.9% a year, while small stocks have eked out annual gains of just 5.6%—and that 5.6% includes 1991's spectacular results.

One of the surest signs of economic recovery is job growth. Small cap companies should be one of the leading forces here because, for the past several years, they have provided much of the job growth in the United States. While large companies such as Boeing and IBM down-sized their work force during the 1980's and early 1990's, smaller companies such as Microsoft, Inc. have increased their employee base. In contrast to the 1980's, new and emerging companies are where job growth is today in America and where it is expected to remain over the next decade.

Because of their growth orientation, small cap stocks nearly always trade at a premium to the overall market. The premium has generally ranged from 15% to 25%.

Often, the terms *small cap stocks* and *aggressive growth stocks* are used interchangeably, particularly when used in the context of describing a certain type of mutual fund. However, there is a difference between these two types of equities. Aggressive growth funds employ such trading strategies as margining positions and using options as well as futures contracts. Small cap funds do not employ such speculative methods.

Small Cap Track Record

The track record for small cap stocks over several different periods of time are shown in the following table. These returns are average *annual* rates of return for the period ending 12/31/91 (for example, the *1-year* period is for the 1991 calendar year). These are the rates of return that you can expect most frequently.

Average Annualized *Rates of Return*

Period	Return
1 Year	+17.1%
3 Years	+15.9%
5 Years	+15.5%
10 Years	+15.1%
20 Years	+14.4%

Even though this category of stocks performed quite well during most of these periods, look at the following table. It shows the *worst* performing period during each of several different time frames over the past 20 years.

Worst Annualized *Rates of Return*

Period	Return
3 Years	−16.7%
5 Years	−12.2%
10 Years	+ 3.2%
15 Years	+ 5.9%
20 Years	+ 8.2%

As a point of interest, over the past 50 years, there have been only two periods where small cap stocks had two or more negative years consecutively: 1969–1970 and 1973–74. Considering the upside potential, this "worst case" situation is quite comforting.

For sake of comparison, let us now look at the single *best* performing period for each of these same blocks of time:

Best* Annualized *Rates of Return

Period	Return
3 Years	+71.3%
5 Years	+45.1%
10 Years	+30.4%
15 Years	+23.3%
20 Years	+21.3%

Finally, you may want to see how small cap stocks have performed over one, three, five, 10, 20, and 50 years. Thus, *1 year* in the following table shows returns for the 1991 calendar year, *3 years* covers the period 1989–1991, and so on.

Average* Annualized *Rates of Return

Period	Return
1 Year	+44.6%
3 Years	+ 11.1%
5 Years	+ 9.4%
10 Years	+ 13.9%
20 Years	+ 17.5%
50 Years	+20.1%

As you can see, the good years greatly outshine the bad years. If you are a statistician or gambler, you may appreciate the following table. It shows, over the last 50 years ending 12/31/92, the odds of someone making money in small cap stocks, depending upon their holding period.

Historical Odds of Obtaining Certain Annual Rates of Return (0, 6, 10, & 15%)

Over This Period	Percentage of Time Annual Returns Were Greater Than			
	0%	6%	10%	15%
1 Year	72%	64%	60%	54%
3 Years	88%	73%	63%	54%
5 Years	96%	89%	76%	43%
10 Years	100%	90%	83%	49%
15 Years	100%	97%	92%	50%
20 Years	100%	100%	94%	39%

As an example, when the table describes "Over 1 Year Period of Time," this means that the chances of your making a 15% (or greater) return was 56%, had you chosen a year at random over the past half century (for example, 1946, 1977, 1985, and 1990). The "3-Year Period" means the same thing except that a random, but consecutive three years in a row were used (for example, 1963–1965, 1971–1973, and 1987–1989). The same can be said for any of the time periods described in this table.

Small stocks have done better under Democrats, looking at the performance of big-company and small-company stocks under Republican and Democratic administrations. For the larger stocks, there was little difference: Big-company issues rose an average of 5% a year under Republicans, and 5.8% a year under Democrats.

But for small-company stocks, the difference was striking. They rose an average of 12.7% a year under Democrats, and fell 2.6% a year under Republicans.

Small cap stocks represent a new investment category for most investors. Often, lack of familiarity translates into fear. This is true when it comes to small cap, aggressive growth, foreign equities, and international securities.

Performance

Historical returns over the past three, five, 10 and 15 years for aggressive growth and small company stock funds are shown in the following table. All of the figures shown in the table below are average *annual* rates of return.

Category	Years 3	5	10	15
Aggressive Growth	20%	11%	14%	15%
Small Company Stocks	19%	14%	13%	16%
S & P 500	16%	11%	18%	15%

One of the features offered by most mutual funds is dollar-cost averaging. This method of investing eliminates much of the extremes that are sometimes experienced by not only small cap stocks, but by bonds and blue chip issues as well.

Dollar-Cost Averaging

Dollar-cost averaging (DCA) is a simple, yet effective, way to reduce risk, whether you are investing in stocks or bonds. The premise behind dollar-cost averaging is that if several purchases of a fund are made over an extended period of time, the unpredictable highs and lows will "average out." The investor ends up with buying some shares at a comparatively low price, others at perhaps a much higher price.

DCA assumes that investors are willing to sacrifice the possibility of having bought all of their shares at the lowest price, in return for knowing that they did not also buy every share at the highest price. In short, we are willing to accept a compromise; a sort of *risk-adjusted* decision.

DCA is based on investing a fixed amount of money in a given fund at specific intervals. Typically, an investor will add a few hundred dollars at the beginning of each month into the XYZ mutual fund. DCA works best if you invest and continue to invest on a pre-established schedule, *regardless of price fluctuations.* You will be buying more shares when the price is down than when it is up. Most investors do not mind buying shares when prices are increasing, since this means that their existing shares are also going up. When this program is followed, losses during market declines are limited, while the ability to participate in good markets is maintained.

Another advantage of DCA is that it increases the likelihood that you will follow an investment program. Like other aspects of our life, it is important to have goals and objectives.

Example of Dollar-Cost Averaging ($1,000 Invested Per Period)

Period (1)	Price of Security (2)	Number of Shares Bought with $1000 (3)	Total Shares Owned (3) (4)	Total Amount Invested (5)	Current Value of Shares (2)x(4) (6)	Net Gain or Loss Percentage (6)/(5) (7)
1	$100	10.0	10.0	$1,000	$1,000	0
2	80	12.5	22.5	2,000	1,800	−10.0
3	70	14.3	36.8	3,000	2,576	−14.1
4	60	16.7	53.5	4,000	3,210	−19.7
5	50	20.0	73.5	5,000	3,675	−26.5
6	70	14.3	87.8	6,000	6,146	+2.4
7	80	12.5	100.3	7,000	8,024	−14.6
8	100	10.0	110.3	8,000	11,030	+37.9

Alger

Since its inception in 1986, the Alger Small Capitalization Portfolio has specialized in growth equity management. Their philosophy has remained unchanged since the beginning: Superior returns by investing in rapidly growing companies with market capitalizations below $1 billion. Whenever possible, the firm buys shares of vital creative companies that provide goods or services to what is expected to be a growing marketplace. From time to time, Alger will also own interests in companies undergoing a life cycle change (such as management, acquisition, and so on), which should lead to higher earnings.

Alger has an internal staff of 20 research personnel. One of the company's distinguishing features is that they do all of their own research and do not sell such research to anyone else. An important benefit of doing one's own research is that the investment process can continually be improved and refined; something you can't do if you are buying outside research. Their research library is unequalled when it comes to information about smaller corporations.

Over the past decade, Alger has developed a comprehensive in-house training program. This program allows the firm's research associates to progress in responsibility and move up through the different levels of analyst positions. Today, there are several leading mutual fund managers throughout the industry who were trained in this program.

This investment philosophy and strategy have produced the following results from Alger Small Capitalization Portfolio for the period ending 12/31/92:

1987	− 1.5%
1988	+ 17.5%
1989	+ 64.5%
1990	+ 6.7%
1991	+ 54.6%
1992	+ 4%

Average annualized rates of return for the past 3 and 5 years have been 19.7% and 27.1% respectively. The fund's only negative year, 1987, was also the year of the stock market crash.

In addition to their small cap fund, Alger also offers the following mutual fund portfolios: growth, balanced, income and growth, and money market. The small cap fund appears in the 1993 section of *The 100 Best Mutual Funds You Can Buy* (their money market fund has appeared in every edition of the book).

For additional information, prospectus, and application, call (800) 992-3863, or write to:

The Alger Fund
30 Montgomery Street, 13th Floor
Jersey City, NJ 07302

Summary

No matter what legislation passes during Clinton's first few years, smaller companies will either be benefactories of such programs or at least not be as harmed by them as big business. President Clinton's inaugural address used the word "change" 11 times. Smaller companies can react more swiftly to change than big corporations. Equally important, some of the costs that will be passed on to corporate America, thereby easing federal involvement and expense, will be avoided by most of the small businesses through exemptions or credits.

As you can see, investing in small cap or aggressive growth stocks can be much safer than one might initially suspect. Dollar-cost averaging means that your purchases are spread out over an extended period of time; a drop in share prices translates into more shares purchased for the same amount of money the following month, higher share prices mean that existing shares are appreciating. "Percolating" into a fund like this makes sense for skeptical investors, even though this sector of the market is once again receiving rave reviews.

More than any other investment described in this book, small cap stocks have the potential for turning in exciting returns for the next several years.

7

Foreign Equities

As an investor, you are probably aware that investments are somewhat cyclical in nature. Bonds perform well for a while, then stocks lead the pack, often followed by real estate and occasionally money market instruments. As clear as these general trends appear in hindsight, the great majority of people never seem to get in at the ground level. In fact, you may be surprised to learn that most investors buy at the top of a market, be it stocks, bonds, metals, or real estate, and sell at the bottom. The instincts of greed and fear are quite strong.

Well, you now have a chance to get in at the ground floor, during the next recovery. I am not talking about investing in the Dow Jones Industrial Average; instead, I am talking about foreign stocks.

Last year, 1992, marked the fourth year in a row that international stocks, as a general category, under-performed their US counterparts. It is not very common that this happens even two years in a row. This has been the only time that it has happened four times back to back over the past quarter of a century. Why would you want to invest in such "losers?" Well, as Sir John Templeton, the grandfather of mutual funds and global investing has constantly said, "Invest in places where the pessimism is the greatest." The Templeton Growth Fund has outperformed any investment you can think of over the past 30+ years

If you doubt the soundness of such a statement, merely look at recent events. The US was at the height of its recession in 1991, yet our stock markets posted one of their best years ever (the Dow and the S & P 500 were both up over 30%). The press may have shown you story after story about plant closings and large unemployment lines, but gave little attention to what was going on in Wall Street. The same thing is true with China. There was a tremendous scare around the world after Tienenman Square. Hong Kong stocks plummeted. Yet, as this pessimism peaked within just a few weeks after the suppression, the Hong Kong stock market went on to post some incredible gains. And, when China allowed some very limited security trading in late 1992, their people were euphoric, buying every share within a matter of minutes.

Although this is probably not his intent, President Clinton's domestic agenda will greatly benefit the foreign stock markets. As our numbers begin to improve, there will be more and more comparison to our recovery versus the continued recession with our trading partners. This negativism will create buying opportunities for the "smart money" (institutional buyers such as mutual funds and large pension plans). By investing now in mutual funds and unit trusts that own foreign securities, you can participate in these big gains.

There has been a great deal of talk concerning universal health care, job creation, tax credits, rate hikes, and the rebuilding of our infrastructure, but few positive things have been said about investment opportunities abroad. If you are the type of investor who believes that the "cat is out of the bag" concerning US opportunities (that is, that select stocks have already risen due to improved expectations), this chapter will give you some fresh ideas.

US blue chip stocks are near or at all-time highs. The Dow Jones Industrial Average (DJIA) and the Standard & Poor's 500 (S & P 500) have not had a significant negative year since 1981. A good number of financial writers believe that some type of correction is at hand. After all, the great bull market of the 1980's benefited the blue chips. There was only a brief interruption in the later part of 1987. Domestic as well as foreign investment bankers and brokerage firms feel that it is about time for the bull to take a rest perhaps for a year or two.

This is not the case for small cap stocks (see the previous chapter), which suffered a beating in 1990 before taking off in 1991 and having an uneventful year in 1992. The decade of the 1980's seemed to almost forget about small cap stocks. This sector of US stocks, which normally outperforms the large, blue chip issues, enjoyed only about a third of the returns that large cap stocks experienced.

Because small cap stocks are usually much more volatile than blue chip stocks, US investors have been reluctant to commit more than a nominal amount to this area. However, as you will see later in this chapter, US stocks, when coupled with foreign equities can result in a portfolio that has much less risk and higher returns than one comprised of US equities alone, whether those equities are small or large cap. Let us begin with an overview of the world marketplace.

Global Perspective: Winners Everywhere

Over the past decade, an integrated world economy has evolved from the many distinct national economies of the past. At the same time, many investment opportunities, once considered uniquely American, have gradually shifted to other areas around the globe. With 62% of today's stock market capitalization represented by non-US companies, the case for globally diversifying your portfolio has never been stronger. To earn competitive returns, US investors can no longer afford to ignore foreign opportunities.

Increasing your investment returns and reducing portfolio risk are two compelling reasons for investing world-wide. Global investing allows you to maximize your returns by investing in some of the world's best-managed and most profitable companies. Japan, for example, is the world's leading producer of sophisticated electronics goods; Germany, heavy machinery; the United States, biotechnology; and Southeast Asia, commodity-manufactured goods.

World market dominance is constantly changing. Ten years ago, the US represented half of the world's stock market capital, but today it represents only one-third of total world capitalization. Only twice in the past 10 years has the US stock market been among the five best performers in the world.

World Stock Market Capitalization

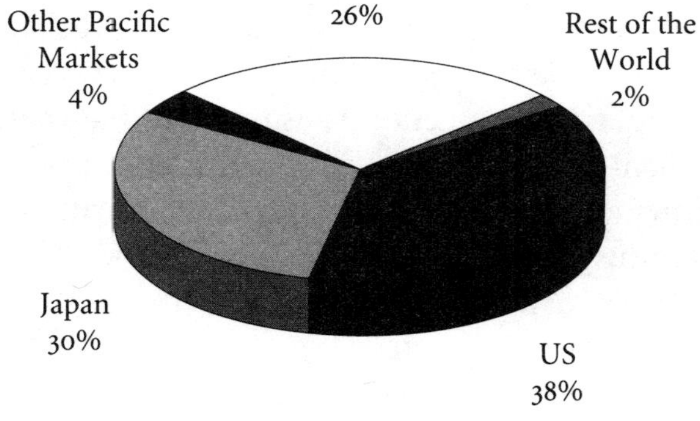

SOURCE: MORGAN STANLEY CAPITAL INTERNATIONAL, DECEMBER 31, 1991

Historically, US investors found ample investment opportunity right here in the US. And carefully selected companies still offer superior potential for increased returns. In fact, among the nations providing the most potential for growth today are those that are industrializing, have the cheapest labor and richest natural resources, and yet remain undervalued.

Pacific Basin

The Pacific Region, which includes Japan, Hong Kong, Korea, Taiwan, Thailand, Singapore, Malaysia, and Australia, has experienced outstanding economic growth and today represents 34% of the world's stock market capital—nearly double what it was 10 years ago.

Japan, the most economically mature country in the Pacific Basin, has become the dominant force behind the development of the newly industrialized countries (NICs) of Hong Kong, Korea, Thailand, Singapore, Malaysia, and Taiwan. As demand for Japanese products has grown and costs in Japan have risen, the search for affordable production of goods has caused Japanese investment to flow into neighboring countries, fostering their development as economically independent and prosperous nations.

The NICs, with some of the cheapest world labor forces and richest untapped natural resources, have recently experienced an enormous influx of international investment capital and today represent the world's fastest growing source of low-cost manufacturing. These newly industrialized countries are favored locations for the manufacturing and assembly of consumer electronics products. Displaced from high-cost countries, such as the US and Japan, electronics factories in these developing countries significantly benefit from reduced labor costs. Today, in fact, Korea is the world's third largest manufacturer of semiconductors.

The Pacific Region yields yet another country with the potential for strong economic growth: China. Opportunities to benefit from the industrialization of China will come from firms listed on the Hong Kong stock exchange in such basic areas as electricity, construction materials, public transportation, and fundamental telecommunications. These low technology and essential industries, once growth industries in the United States, are now the foundation of a natural growth progression occurring in the NICs of Southeast Asia.

Companies such as China Light and Power (Hong Kong), Siam Cement (Thailand), and Hyundai (Korea) offer much the same profit potential today as their northern European counterparts did 100 years ago, their US counterparts 40 years ago, and their Japanese counterparts as early as 20 years ago.

Pacific Basin Stock Market Returns

10 Years Ended December 31, 1992

Thailand	31.5%
Korea	20.0%
Japan	16.4%
Hong Kong	25.5%
Australia	15.3%
Singapore/Malaysia	9.5%

Europe

Investors have long been familiar with the names of many of Europe's major producers—Nestlé, Olivetti, Shell, Bayer, Volkswagen, and Perrier, to name just a few. Europe's impressive manufacturing capacity, diverse industrial base, quality labor pools, and its many leading multinational blue chip corporations can make it an environment for growth, accessible to you through foreign funds.

European markets have proven time and again that they represent tremendous investment potential. Over the past 10 years, European markets have consistently produced greater total returns than the US stock market.

European Stock Market Returns

10 Years Ended December 31, 1992	
Austria	20.3%
Belgium	25.4%
Denmark	14.4%
France	23.1%
Germany	16.4%
Italy	14.3%
Netherlands	22.1%
Norway	16.5%
Spain	20.9%
Sweden	17.6%
Switzerland	17.0%
UK	17.9%
US	16.0%

Although recent European market returns have been disappointing, these markets are due to turn around. The astounding political and economic changes in western Germany have led the Bundesbank to keep interest rates high to pay for the rebuilding of infrastructure in eastern Germany. Other European nations, bound by the exchange rate limitations of the new European Community economic accords, have had to maintain artificially high interest rates. As the pressures of paying for German reunification ease, German interest rates should begin to decline and spur economic growth. This trend should lead to similar patterns throughout Europe.

With economic deregulation and the elimination of internal trade barriers, many European companies are—for the first time in history—investing in and competing for exposure to the whole European market. Companies that are currently restricted to manufacturing and distributing within their national boundaries will soon be able to locate facilities anywhere in Europe, maximizing the efficient employment of labor, capital and raw materials.

As you can see from the 1992 table below, the elimination of trade barriers creates a single economy that compares favorably to the United States.

	Europe	US
Population	334 million	250 million
Total GDP	$6.3 trillion	$5.4 trillion
Market Capitalization	$2.6 trillion	$3.7 trillion
Trade Balance	–$388 million	$108 billion

SOURCES: G.T. CAPITAL MANAGEMENT, BLOOMBERG, INTERNATIONAL FINANCIAL STATISTICS, AND MORGAN STANLEY CAPITAL INTERNATIONAL

World Market Performance

Fifteen of the 20 largest corporations in the world are located outside of the United States. It just makes sense to invest in these and other corporations and industries to take advantage of opportunities wherever they appear. To get an idea of this return potential, look at the following table. See how the US has fared compared to stocks markets in other countries. Notice that the US ranked eleventh over the past 10 years. All of the figures shown are adjusted for any good or bad foreign currency swings (meaning that these percentage figures reflect those times when the US dollar has been strong *and* weak).

Annualized Returns, ***10 Years Ended December 31, 1991***

Rank	US Dollar Returns
1 Thailand	35.5%
2 Hong Kong	25.5%
3 Belgium	25.4%
4 France	23.1%
5 Netherlands	22.1%
11 US	16.0%

1993–1999 Outlook for Europe and the Pacific Region

The pressure in Europe to slash interest rates over the next one or two years could trigger dramatic stock rallies there, just as similar US rate cuts in 1990 helped push 1991 returns here to over 30%. And although Japan remains a swamp for investors, the Pacific Rim's emerging markets combine low-stock multiples with vigorous economic growth that could drive prices up as much as 25% next year.

That's why financial advisors are urging Americans to allocate at least 20% of their total portfolios in 1993 to foreign holdings, focusing on Europe and Southeast Asia. These regions offer better profit potential than the US, not only for 1993 but also for the longer term.

The biggest financial story of the decade will be the opening of China to world markets and, to a lesser degree, the economic unification of Europe. Now is the time for investors to get in on these events.

The eight "tigers" of the Pacific Rim: Hong Kong, Indonesia, Korea, Malaysia, the Philippines, Singapore, Taiwan, and Thailand—carry a modest multiple of 14 times estimated 1993 profits. While the Pacific Rim may deliver 1993's greatest overall gain, money managers have lately been finding a lot of individual bargains in Europe. Shares there are trading at an average price/earning index of only 11, since investors are concerned that Europe's economic slowdown may be longer and harsher than government forecasts suggest.

Performance

If you were to construct a grid of the top performing stock markets around the world, ranked first through fifth place covering the past 11 years, you would have a total of 66 different slots. On this entire grid, the US would appear only twice. In 1982 the United States had the second best performing stock market in the world; in 1991 it was ranked third, as shown in the following table.

Top-Performing Markets 1982–1992 (In US Dollars)

Year	1st	2nd	3rd	4th	5th
1982	Sweden 24%	US 22%	Netherlands 17%	Germany 10%	Belgium 10%
1983	Norway 82%	Denmark 69%	Australia 56%	Sweden 50%	Netherlands 38%
1984	Hong Kong 47%	Spain 42%	Japan 17%	Belgium 13%	Netherlands 12%
1985	Austria 177%	Germany 137%	Italy 134%	Switzerland 108%	France 83%
1986	Spain 123%	Italy 109%	Japan 100%	Belgium 81%	France 79%
1987	Japan 43%	Spain 38%	UK 35%	Canada 15%	Denmark 14%
1988	Belgium 55%	Denmark 54%	Sweden 49%	Norway 43%	France 39%
1989	Austria 105%	Germany 47%	Norway 46%	Denmark 45%	Sing./Mal. 42%
1990	UK 10%	Hong Kong 9%	Austria 7%	Norway 1%	Denmark 0%
1991	Hong Kong 50%	Australia 36%	US 31%	Sing./Mal. 25%	New Zealand 21%
1992	Hong Kong 32%	Switzer-land 32%	US 7%	Sing./Mal. 6%	Netherlands 21%

SOURCE: MORGAN STANLEY CAPITAL INTERNATIONAL

Historical returns over the past three, five, 10 and 15 years for global stock funds are shown in the following table (for periods ending 12/31/92). All of the figures shown in the table are average *annual* rates of return.

Category	Years			
Category	3	5	10	15
Global Stock Funds (Includes US)	1.7%	7.6%	12.7%	16.0%
Foreign Stock Funds	–1%	−1.9%	5.8%	13.2%
S & P 500	10.8%	16.1%	16.2%	16.0%

Risk Reduction

Like any other investment, this one should not be looked at in a vacuum. The real beauty of foreign funds shines through when they are combined with other categories of US equities. According to a Stanford University study, one's overall risk level is cut in half when a *global* portfolio of stocks is used instead of one based on US issues alone. And, as already demonstrated, returns are also greater when we look for opportunities worldwide instead of just domestically.

It's commonly known that diversification reduces investment risk. Recent studies have once again proven this most basic investment principle. One study showed that the least volatile investment portfolio would be composed of 60% US equities and 40% foreign equities. These results reflect the importance of balancing a portfolio between US and foreign equities.

Global Diversification Reduces Risk

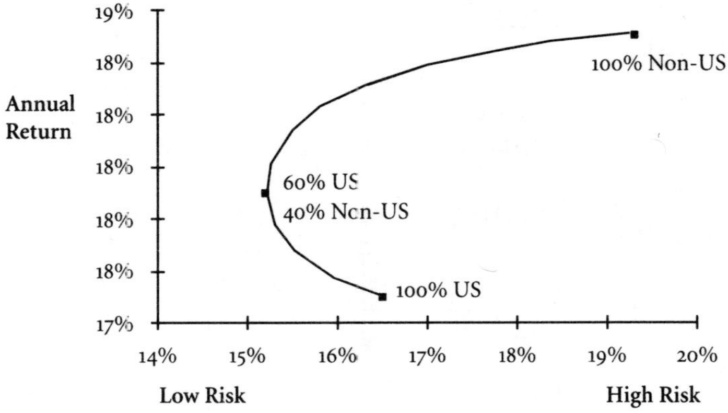

Mutual Funds

International funds invest only in stocks of foreign companies, while global funds invest in both foreign and US stocks. It is wise to consider investing abroad, since different economies experience prosperity and recession at different times. During the 1980's, foreign stocks were the number one performing investment, averaging a compound return of over 22% per year, versus 17% for US stocks and 9% for residential real estate.

Also known as *foreign funds*, this category of mutual funds invests in equities issued by international firms. Some foreign funds are broadly diversified, including stocks from European as well as Pacific Basin economies. Other international funds specialize in a particular region or country. Global, also known as *world*, stock funds can invest in any country. The more countries a fund can invest in, the lower its overall risk level will be; often, return potential will also increase.

Most US investors have never been in an international or global fund. A good way to get your feet wet is by going into the SoGen International Fund. This fund has an excellent track record (shown in the next table), which placed it in the top 15% of all mutual funds over the past 10 and 15 years. This is quite a feat when you consider that the fund has experienced only 30% of the risk that other growth funds have gone through.

SoGen

SoGen International Fund began operations in 1970. The fund's adviser is SGTR Corporation, an indirect subsidiary of Societe Generale, a major French bank. Jean-Marie Eveillard has been Portfolio Manager of SoGen International Fund since 1979.

The fund's investment approach is generally risk-averse by diversifying among a variety of financial instruments. The fund invests in stocks and fixed-income securities, both in the United States and in foreign markets.

In terms of specific security selection, the emphasis is on value, that is, when the current price of a security is low in relation to the appraisal of its worth. The fund is often drawn toward depressed securities of larger corporations and toward the securities of relatively small and obscure companies. The idea is that the lesser known a company, the more likely the possibility that its securities are mispriced by the market.

Value investing is a well-known technique in the United States, but it is seldom applied by foreign investors in their local markets. Since growth and momentum investors dominate these stock exchanges, securities that appeal to value buyers, such as SoGen, are unwanted or ignored by locals. The result is abundant opportunity for the global bargain hunter.

SoGen International Fund was one of 19 funds listed on the honor roll in the August 31, 1992 edition of *Forbes.* The fund was selected on the bases of its long-term performance, down-market performance, consistency of results, and continuity of management. The fund also receives top marks in every edition of the book, *The 100 Best Mutual Funds You Can Buy.*

Year	Total Return
1992	+ 8.4
1991	+ 17.9
1990	− 1.3
1989	+ 17.2
1988	+ 14.1
1987	+ 13.7
1986	+ 25.0
1985	+ 32.7
1984	+ 2.7
1983	+ 24.0
1982	+ 31.6
1981	+ 8.0
1980	+ 31.7
1979	+ 24.1
1978	+ 7.2
1977	+ 2.3
1976	+ 14.4
1975	+ 26.1
1974	− 21.31
1973	− 20.6
1972	+ 11.7
1971	+ 21.6
1970*	+ 12.3%

*The fund's inception was April 20, 1970.

When reviewing these figures, keep in mind the following points:

- The fund has only had three negative years since its inception.
- Jean-Marie Eveillard has only experienced one negative year (off 1.3% in 1990) since he became the fund's manager in 1979.

Maximum Current with Minimum Risk

One of the best ways to safely increase your current income and have a hedge against inflation is what is known as a *systematic withdrawal program (SWP)*. These programs can be set up through mutual funds, variable annuity families, or both. You and your investment advisor decide which types of investment categories are best suited for you based on time, risk level, tax bracket and desired level of income.

Money is then invested into each one of these categories. Accounts are structured so that all dividends, interest, and capital gains are automatically reinvested. A systematic withdrawal section on the application (sometimes it is a separate supplemental application) is then completed. The SWP part of the application asks when the income stream is to commence (immediately, six months from now, and so on), the dollar amount you want (for example, $120 each month), and the frequency of payments (such as monthly, quarterly, and so on).

An SWP using global funds provides you with a regular income that you can depend on. With money market funds or CDs, you are at the mercy of interest rates and are controlled by what someone is willing to offer you. Bonds pay a set rate, but are not considered hedges against inflation. An equity-based SWP will pay you more income than bonds, can be altered to provide more income at any time in the future, and has historically been an excellent hedge against inflation.

So far, an SWP may sound too good to be true. After all, we are talking about this type of an investment:

- It sends us a monthly check.
- The checks are greater than what our bonds are paying.
- The amount of the checks does not vary unless we contact the mutual fund or variable annuity and request an increase or decrease.
- There is no cost or fee to set up an SWP.
- There is no cost or fee to change, suspend, or reactivate the SWP.
- It is a risk-reduction tool (if more than one type of fund or portfolio is used).

At this point, you are probably saying to yourself, "What's the catch?" To see what the negatives of an SWP are, look at the 10-year example using the SoGen International Fund, following. Study the "Market Value" column carefully; notice that the principal goes up and down. This fluctuation is the price that you will pay. To be effective, and make sure you do not go broke, an SWP must be flexible: The withdrawal rate should be less or on parity with the total return of the fund. This last point is not particularly important for a short-term horizon of five years or less, but must be seriously taken into account if you expect the program to last your remaining lifetime.

Systematic Withdrawal Plan Example

The following table assumes an initial investment of $100,000 in a conservative fund, SoGen. All dividends and capital gains have been reinvested. Since the investor is "income oriented," the account has been structured for a 12% annual withdrawal (based on the value of the account each year this is why the following "Withdraw" figures fluctuate). Withdrawals of 1.00% beginning 10/31/82 and every month thereafter are sent to the investor.

Month End	Withdraw	Market Value	Shares
9/82		$98,000	7,379
12/82	3,273	110,340	7,160
12/83	14,711	122,208	7,415
12/84	13,836	111,700	7,972
12/85	14,903	131,362	7,951
12/86	17,638	145,641	8,223
12/87	19,755	146,880	8,914
12/88	18,076	148,686	8,914
12/89	18,426	154,470	8,663
12/90	17,461	135,115	8,233
12/91	16,929	141,002	7,785
9/92	12,787	139,903	7,112
Total	**$167,795**	**139,903**	**7,112**

Notes: (1) Only $ 4,609 of the cumulative amount withdrawn was subject to capital gains taxes. (2) The annual internal rate of return during this 10-year withdrawal period was 19.1%. (3) Even though $167,795 was taken out (and presumably spent by the investor), the original $100,000 investment has still grown to $139,903.

If you are not certain whether you can live with such variability, ask yourself if you can live with the variability of the continually increasing prices you are paying for everything you purchase. Ask yourself if you invest $100,000 in a bank CD or government bond what the purchasing power of your $100,000 will be when the instrument matures in two, five, 10 or 20 years from now? Equally important, what will the *income* from such investments be able to purchase in five or 10 years? The answer is probably somewhere between one-half to two-thirds of what you are currently consuming. Do you really want your standard of living to decrease by 30 to 50% *every* five to 10 years?

If the concept of an SWP appeals to you, have your financial advisor contact several mutual funds (or variable annuities) and ask for examples. In order to make sure that you are not looking at an artificially good period of time, get examples (known as *hypotheticals* by mutual fund and variable annuity groups) that show performance and withdrawals for at least a 10-year period of time. Remember, you cannot hide bad results if lengthy periods of time are used.

The amount of income you should request under an SWP depends on the caliber of the mutual funds you have chosen. Bond funds, as an example, cannot be expected to pay you 8–12% a year and have any type of net growth to offset inflation. The stock fund you have selected may have averaged 20% a year over the past decade, but do not expect those types of returns for the next 10 or 20 years.

An SWP works best if equity positions (aggressive growth, small cap, growth, growth and income, and international) within a mutual fund or variable annuity family are used. If you do your homework properly, you can structure an 8–14% annual-income stream. The closer you get to taking out 14% per year the less growth of principal you will have, the more you tone down the current income, for example, by staying at nine or 10 percent, the greater your principal will grow.

Some people set up an SWP in the 14–16% range because they desperately need a high level of income to live on. For these people, principal erosion is not a concern because they are not expecting to live for a long time or because they are expecting other sources of income or principal in the future (for example, an inheritance, or the sale of a building, home, or business).

Most people who set up an SWP have a finite portfolio that they must depend on for income for the rest of their lives, which may be 30 or 40 more years. These people should start with an annual income stream in the 9–11% range for a couple of years; this range is lower than what stocks have historically returned. As their comfort level or needs change, either due to investment experience or the effects of inflation, this figure can always be adjusted upwards later. A conservative start means that there will be even greater growth of principal, which means a larger base to take out much more money from later.

Summary

During 1993, you will be seeing some rather dismal trade, unemployment, and growth figures from Europe. The Pacific Basin will show good numbers, but only by US standards. Do not let these negative reports sway you away from investing overseas, remember Templeton's words: "Invest where the pessimism is the greatest."

Large cap US stocks are at or near all-time highs. As a whole, foreign stock markets have not yet enjoyed such peaks in recent years. As an investor, you have the opportunity to buy international equities at some very fair prices.

While the US press focuses on US unemployment figures, job creation, interest rates, and the Dow, little attention will be given to the stock markets overseas. And, just as before, the vast majority of US investors will miss the boat. Armed with the information contained in this chapter, one could say that your ship has just come in. Now you know: A global portfolio of US and foreign securities provides less risk and greater return than one comprised solely of US stocks and bonds.

If you are like most of the financial writers out there who feel that blue chip stocks have enjoyed too much appreciation without any sustained bear market, then foreign equities are for you. Historically, foreign stocks have outperformed their US brethren. Yet, over the past four years, this has not been the case. Therefore, just like small cap stocks, which under-performed the Dow during the 1980's, the time for international investing is now. Most investors buy high and sell low. Wouldn't it be nice to buy into something that is not at historic highs? Foreign stocks, as well as global and international stock funds, offer bargains that are not as readily available in the US.

8

Leasing Programs

Treasury Secretary Bentson has been a friend of business for a number of years. While tax rates go up and the financial burden shared by the states increase, President Clinton and his Treasury Secretary will be encouraging businesses to spend money. There are two ways you can benefit from these incentives:

- Be the owner of a business that ends up receiving some type of tax package.
- Invest in equipment that will benefit from these tax incentives.

At the foundation of the Clinton economic plan is job creation and economic stimulus. At the heart of this plan is the Investment Tax Credit (ITC). The ITC will give the private sector incentives to go out and invest in new plants and equipment, and to increase its capacity to hire. Like other tax credits, the ITC would reduce a company's taxes if it does what the government wants. The government, for instance, might offer a $100 tax break for every $1,000 spent on equipment. Such a step would spur businesses to buy more equipment, stimulating the economy in the near term while encouraging the investments that will make the US more productive in the long run. Such a credit, however, would reduce government receipts about $30 billion a year in the short run.

An ITC is not something new, it was first introduced by President Kennedy. As you can see by the following ITC status table, this form of economic stimulus has been used, suspended, and eliminated by several presidents over the years.

Many studies show that ITCs do stimulate capital spending. But whether they are powerful enough to lift an entire economy has never been proven conclusively. The Kennedy tax credit took affect in 1962 when a recovery was already underway. It was repealed during the Nixon Administration because the economy appeared to be growing too rapidly, and re-established in 1971, again when a brief recession was already ending.

The recession that began in 1974 prompted President Gerald Ford and Congress to raise the credit to 10 percent from seven percent, but the new rate took effect in 1975, when the recession was ending. The 10 percent credit was still in effect during the 1981–82 recession and made little if any difference during the subsequent recovery. After the credit was ended in 1986, attempts during the Bush Administration to revive a version of it were included in the bills Mr. Bush vetoed because the proposed legislation included measures unacceptable to the president.

Date	Status of ITC
January 1962	7% Credit Instituted
October 1966	Credit Suspended
March 1967	7% Credit Reinstated
April 1969	Credit Eliminated
April 1971	7% Credit Instituted
January 1975	Credit Increased to 10%
January 1986	Credit Eliminated

SOURCE: AMERICAN COUNCIL FOR CAPITAL FORMATION

The reinstatement of the ITC will be most beneficial to the manufacturers of equipment. Even though a great number of companies will benefit from such new purchases, these tax savings will be pale when compared against the increased sales of business equipment, machinery, and transportation vehicles. As an investor, you can reap the benefits from such activity by participating in a company that specializes in equipment leasing.

Equipment Lease Defined

Equipment leasing starts with a corporation (lessee) that has a need for a particular type of equipment, such as a forklift or marine shipping container, but does not want to outlay capital to buy the equipment. The lessee may be a Fortune 500 corporation, major steamship line, or other credit-worthy company. The corporation may go to a leasing company (lessor) to attempt to negotiate a lease, or rental agreement, for the equipment.

The lessor may be a leasing company, bank, insurance company, or a professionally managed direct investment. This process may be compared to negotiating a loan with a bank in a purchase scenario. Lease negotiations focus on lease rates (rent) and length of time the contract will be in place (term). When the terms of the lease are finalized, the equipment is delivered to the lessee. The lessee pays rent to the lessor for the right to use the equipment and at the end of the lease term, may extend the lease, buy the equipment, or return the equipment to the lessor in good condition. Equipment leasing is a $125 billion-per-year industry. Banks, insurance companies, and major leasing companies lease capital equipment to credit-worthy companies.

Advantages of the Lease

Today's corporations are exceedingly concerned with their balance sheets, particularly the level of outstanding debt. This is understandable because the stock market's view of company performance is partly based on statistics derived from the balance sheet. When a company finances the purchase of equipment through bank borrowing, the level of debt shown on the balance sheet increases and in turn, decreases future borrowing capacity. This affects the firm's ability to raise money and makes it less flexible in dealing with future events that require additional capital.

Leasing provides off balance sheet financing and eliminates debt that can burden a company. A second advantage to the lessee is that interest rates on debt transactions, the actual cash outflow (rent) to the leasing company (equipment owner), is less, due to the fact that there are no cash payments toward principle pay down. Generally, the entire lease payment can be written off as a monthly operating expense, while in a debt transaction, only the interest portion of the payment can be deducted. In summary, the lessee remains flexible and can easily change, update, or augment the company's equipment as the needs and goals of the firm change.

Advantages to You as an Investor

The fundamental benefit of leasing is the high income that it immediately produces. Instead of paying money market rates for the first several months or years of the program, the lease format produces income soon after the money is invested. Many leasing programs have paid from 10%–12% in the first year and a total *after-tax rate* of return over the life of the program of 10%–13%.

Some of the exceptional programs average 17–20% cash flow throughout the life of the program. Cash flow distributions can be maintained at this level because each payment is part principal and part interest. The aforementioned partial return of principal, combined with the depreciation of the leased assets can provide a 90–100% tax shelter for the income produced by the program for the first five to six years. This increases the taxable equivalent yield of the program to 15–18%.

Inflation Hedge

Equipment leasing also produces a hedge against inflation. When inflation is present, the cost of goods and services increase, thereby making the return from a dollar investment worth less in real terms. For example, a 10-year maturity bond that bears an eight percent coupon will pay $80 a year for 10 years and then return principal. The return of principal after 10 years will buy much less, thus reducing the real amount of investor return. In an equipment-leasing program, the amount of principal returned at the end of the program is reduced by depreciation, but is hedged against inflation. When inflation is high, the cost of equipment (and the monthly payments) goes up and consequently so does the value of used equipment. The equipment can be sold for more, making it a hedge against inflation.

Equipment-leasing Partnerships

Equipment-leasing partnerships that invest in low technology like marine shipping containers are the current stars of the equipment-leasing partnership business. Investors can understand low-technology deals. They have a much easier time identifying with the transportation-related or container equipment partnership.

Equipment-leasing programs, which are designed to provide current income, still can offer some tax advantages through passive losses. What's good about equipment leasing versus other leases and partnerships, is that equipment leasing provides a dependable and predictable income stream. Equipment-leasing programs do well in good and bad economies.

Equipment-leasing partnerships purchase equipment, which they lease to earn rental income for investors and any possible tax benefits from the depreciation of property. The partnership usually comes in two forms: A straight-lease arrangement or a *sale-leaseback deal.* The equipment may be bought by the partnership from a company, then immediately leased back a sale-leaseback.

Equipment-leasing partnerships can include anything from cable TV systems to rail cars to aircraft, to medical equipment or forklifts, or shipping containers.

Each partnership can include one kind of equipment or a mix of equipment. The shipping containers category has become the star of the equipment-leasing partnership business due to its low risk and dependable stream of income. The favored area in recent years has become those partnerships that concentrate on low-technology equipment.

Unlike aircraft leasing and medical equipment, shipping containers don't have a built-in obsolescence and therefore, are less risky and complicated to investors. Marine containers deplete at a slower rate than other assets used in equipment-leasing programs, providing cash flow for a greater period.

Low-Risk Equipment Leasing: Cargo Containers

World trade exists because "the right goods are in the wrong place." Intermodal containers are built in standardized 20- and 40-foot lengths. They can be stacked below and above deck on ships, placed on rail cars or trucks. The container's ability to move, with its cargo, from ship to rail to truck, is the key link to today's transportation chain.

Containers enable a load of cargo to move swiftly from shipper to port, through a port, then onto a ship. Speed and efficiency are achieved as containers are quickly unloaded and sped by truck, rail, or both to their destinations. One example: A company in Indiana could have a container picked up, trucked to Chicago, carried by rail to a West Coast port for loading onto a container ship, and expect delivery in Yokohama in just 16 days.

Dry cargo containers (large steel boxes) carry practically anything—from computers and dishes to cotton, tires, beverages, and stereos. Refrigerated containers carry fruits, vegetables, and meats. The containers protect cargo against the elements, other damage, and theft. Cargo is handled only twice—once at loading and once at unloading. Specialized containers carry liquids, gases, and heavy equipment. The time factor in loading and unloading cargo from ships is greatly reduced by the use of containers. Container ships carrying more than 4,000 containers can now unload in a mere 16 hours, instead of the one to two weeks that would be required if the cargo were shipped on pallets.

Huge container ports worldwide employ giant gantry cranes to pluck loaded containers (20 to 30 tons) from shipyard shuttles and place them aboard the ship at the rate of one every two minutes. Other gantries move about the yards to load and unload semi-trailer, trains, and yard shuttles in a minimum of time.

World Trade

Today, changes are taking place in abundance around the world. For the first time since World War II, communism is on the retreat, military dictatorship and civilian governments have given way to democratically elected governments in most major countries. Such changes often set the stage for enormous increases in productivity, foreign investment, industrial output, export activity, and consumer demand for both domestically produced and imported goods, all of which can spur growth in the global economies.

The demand for containers will continue to increase. That confidence is based on several factors. First, world trade has been growing every year since 1983 and is estimated to grow at an annual rate of 3.4% per year between 1990 and the year 2000.

Secondly, the number of containers in service increased from 270,000 in 1969 to over 6.3 million at the end of 1992. The continued internal conversion of cargo from the traditional break-bulk method of shipping to the more efficient containerized method, combined with the increased amount of goods being manufactured and shipped, will require a continued growth in the number of containers in the world.

Every year, more and more of the world's general cargo travels between nations in locked intermodal containers. The shift to containerized shipping that began in the early 1970's is still under way. Every year since 1970, containers have carried more general cargo than the year before. Since it is anticipated that containerized cargo will be the fastest growing segment of global trade over the next 10 years, worldwide demand for containers should continue strong.

The continuing rapid pace of containerization in the late 1980's was funded not just by large increases in trade between industrialized and developing countries, but also by a very sharp rise in the level of traffic between industrialized countries. Growth up to the year 2005 is projected at 77%.

Cronos Global Income Fund

Cronos Containers is one of the 10 largest container-leasing companies in the world, with over 120,000 (20-foot or equivalent) units of dry cargo and refrigerated container equipment under management, and $100 million in annual lease revenues.

The Cronos network consists of over 100 personnel operating from 14 locations throughout the world, who are totally focused on the business of leasing containers. Through this network, Cronos provides leasing services to a customer base of nearly 250 companies engaged in international container transport.

Example of How a Cargo Container Program Works

The Cronos Global Income Fund purchases marine cargo containers and container related equipment for lease in marine transportation (each year the company comes out with a new program, the current program is number XIV). The primary objectives of its direct participation programs are to generate continuing income for the fund's investors and to realize the residual value of the equipment at the end of its useful life.

Should the cost of new containers continue to increase, investors could realize the benefit of any increased rental rates that may also occur. It is also expected that there will be favorable tax consequences during the early years of investment from depreciation, which could shelter 90–100% of all cash distributions for up to six years.

Cronos funds work in four phases: Start-up, reinvestment, distribution, and wind-up. During the *start-up phase* (1993), the general partner (Cronos) purchases containers and then leases them to credit-worthy marine transportation companies. Fully sheltered cash distributions and tax losses depend, in part, on when the investor enters the program. During the *reinvestment phase* (1994–1998), the partnership (also referred to as the "fund" or "program") makes monthly cash distributions and invests in additional equipment. During the *distribution phase* (after 1998), all distributable cash from operations is used for cash distributions. At this point, no additional equipment is purchased. It is during this phase that cash distributions will be their highest. After approximately 10 years of service, the equipment will begin to be sold, usually for storage uses, and the proceeds are distributed to the investors (the limited partners). This is known as the *wind-up phase.* It is anticipated that, by the 15th year, all equipment will be sold and the partnership will be terminated.

To give you a better idea as to how a leasing program looks after a number of years, look at all of Cronos' past public-limited partnerships. As you review the figures in the following table, note the following points:

- Despite the high pay-out on the earlier programs, they still have a life expectancy of several more years.
- Future partnerships could benefit from the reinstatement of the Investment Tax Credit (ITC).
- Cash flow figures (the current yield to investors) should continue to increase.
- Figures for the more recent programs are naturally lower because they have not been in existence as long.
- The amount reinvested means that total return figures (which include the residual value of the containers when they are sold in years 10–15) will be even higher, since each investor owns more containers than originally expected.

Partnership	Date Formed	Distribution	Pay-out to Date	ITC	Amount Reinvested
IEA V (A)	11/83	20%	148%	8%	16%
IEA V (B)	4/84	20%	130%	9%	12%
IEA VI	9/84	27%	131%	7%	19%
IEA VII	12/86	30%	109%	—	24%
IEA VIII	10/87	23%	74%	—	29%
IEA IX	9/88	12%	43%	—	13%
IEA X	11/89	12%	29%	—	1%
IEA XI	12/90	12%	18%	—	N/A
IEA XII	12/91	N/A	N/A	—	N/A

Summary

Clinton has made it very clear that he favors an ITC. Until its final passage, we will not know what individual companies will be able to take advantage of this buying incentive. Fortunately, that is not important. What we do know is that the manufacturers of this equipment will reap additional revenues through increased sales. By being a partial owner in this equipment (as the lessor), you reap these benefits.

Equipment leasing provides some of the highest returns available. By sticking with low-technology, boring equipment such as fork-lifts, construction equipment, and cargo containers, investors will face fewer surprises when the equipment is sold (residual values that the used equipment is eventually sold for) is a key component to the real returns of any leasing program.

Even if the ITC does not benefit the program you are currently in or contemplating, don't let that dissuade you. Leasing programs can be a steady, conservative source of income that can be partially or fully sheltered from income taxes for several years.

9

Fixed-Rate Annuities

DURING THE FIRST TWO YEARS of this new administration, there will be a tremendous amount of uncertainty. No one is certain if long- or short-term rates will go up, how the stock market will react, whether real estate prices will start to recover, or if foreign securities will start to appreciate at the same pace they did during the 1980's. If you don't have a sense of certainty about what will unfold, and you are not comfortable with what *could* happen in the different marketplaces, then fixed-rate annuities are for you.

One thing is certain, the income tax rate for millions of Americans will be going up. No matter what bracket you are in now or in the future, no matter how conservative or aggressive you might be, no matter whether you like domestic securities or their foreign counterparts, there is one investment vehicle that can fulfill all such criteria and protect you from income taxes: an annuity.

An annuity is an *investment* between you and an insurance company. It represents a contractual relationship between you and the company. And, although *offered* only by the insurance industry, annuities do not have anything to do with life or any other type of insurance coverage. Annuities are *marketed* through brokerage firms, insurance agencies, banks, savings and loan institutions, financial planners, and investment advisors. Close to $60 billion worth of annuities were sold last year; sales were close to $50 billion in 1991 and over $35 billion in 1990.

When you purchase, or invest, in an annuity, you are given certain assurances by the insurance company. There are two different types of annuities: *fixed* (a set rate of return) and *variable* (the investor chooses from a series of portfolios that range from conservative to aggressive). This chapter will cover fixed-rate annuities; the following chapter will detail variable annuities.

There are always four parties to each annuity, fixed-rate or variable: the insurer, the contract owner, the annuitant, and the beneficiary. Since annuities represent a new investment for most people and will surely be one of the most popular investments of the 1990's, let us see exactly the function of these parties and what they do.

The Insurer

Whether you invest in an annuity through your local bank, financial planner, brokerage firm, or anyone else who is licensed to sell this product, the agreement is always between you and an insurance company. There are over 2,000 insurance companies in the United States; several hundred of these insurers deal in annuities.

The insurance company you choose, also known as the *insurer*, invests your money. The insurer is always an insurance company. In addition to placing the money, the company makes certain promises. These assurances and the terms of the agreement are contained within the annuity contract. The contract spells out what can and cannot be done. Items such as adding more money, making withdrawals, cancellations, penalties, and guarantees are all spelled out.

Perhaps the best way to explain how the insurer operates is by analogy. When you invest in a bank certificate of deposit (CD), you sign an agreement. If you purchase a mutual fund, you fill out an application. These agreements and contracts are between you and the financial institution. They tell you what your rights and privileges are; they also point out what will happen if you decide not to abide by those terms. When you invest in an annuity you also enter into a similar arrangement; the terms may be different, and the other party is an insurance company, but other than that, it is very similar.

The Contract Owner

The investors in the annuity are known as the *contract owners.* It is their money; they decide among the different options being offered. The contract owner has the right and ability to add more money, terminate the agreement, withdraw part or all of the money, or change the parties named in the contract.

The contract owner can be an individual, couple, trust, corporation, or partnership. The only requirement is that the owner is an adult. A minor can be the owner as long as the policy lists the minor's custodian (for example, "Ellise Hamilton, custodian for the benefit of Timothy Hamilton").

The contract owner is similar to the purchaser of a mutual fund or bank CD. When you buy a mutual fund, you are the owner. You have the right to invest more money, liquidate the entire account, take some or all of the money out, and change the title of the account (its ownership). However, as a contract owner, you must also be aware of the terms of the agreement. If you decide to make additions, withdrawals, or a complete liquidation, there may be restrictions or penalties—a concern that is also shared by a CD or mutual fund investor.

Since contract owners control this investment, they can give or will part or all of the contract to anyone or any entity at any time.

The Annuitant

If there is one party to the annuity that is difficult to understand, it is the *annuitant.* The best way to understand the purpose of the annuitant is also by analogy. When you purchase life insurance, the insured party is named. The life insurance policy continues in force until the owner terminates the contract, fails to make any required premium payments, or the insured dies. An annuity remains in force until the contract owner makes a change or the annuitant dies. Thus, the annuitant is like the "insured" in a life insurance policy.

In essence, the annuitant is simply the measuring life of the annuity. The annuitant, like an insured, has no voice or control of the contract. The annuitant does not have the power to make withdrawals, deposits, change the names of the parties to the agreement, or terminate the contract. And, like purchasing life insurance on someone else (the insured), the annuitant must also sign the annuity contract.

The person you name as the annuitant (the *insured*) can be anyone: your spouse, parent, child, relative, friend, or neighbor. The only qualification is that the named annuitant is actually a person (that is, *not* a living trust, corporation, partnership, and so on) currently living who is under a certain age. The maximum age of the proposed annuitant depends upon the insurance company. Most companies require that the annuitant be under the age of 75 when the contract is initially signed. Other companies set a maximum age of 70 or 80. It is important to note that the contract (the investment) *may* still stay in force after the annuitant reaches the "maximum age."

As previously mentioned, the annuitant has no voice in the control or disposition of the annuity. There is only one situation in which the annuitant can benefit from an annuity. This specific event is known as *annuitization* and is a means of liquidating an account over a number of years. If the period is based on someone's life expectancy or for at least five years, then each payment (monthly, quarterly, semi-annually or annually) is considered to be part interest and part principal. This means that a portion of each check is not taxable. This "tax-free" portion may be a small or very large (such as 80–90%) percentage.

Most annuities allow the contract owner to change the annuitant at any time. The only stipulation is that the new annuitant must have been alive when the contract was originally set up.

The Beneficiary

Like a vice president of a country, the beneficiary is of little value until the death of a certain individual. In the case of an annuity, the beneficiary is *waiting for the death of the annuitant.* And, like the beneficiary of a life insurance policy, the beneficiary of an annuity has no voice in the control or management of the policy. The only way in which the beneficiary can prosper from an annuity is upon the death of the annuitant.

The named beneficiaries can be children, friends, relatives, spouses, neighbors, trusts, corporations, or partnerships. The annuity application allows for multiple beneficiary designations of varying or similar proportions (for example, 25% to Mary Jones, 15% to Jack Jones, 10% to Edward Smith, and 50% to the Nelson Family Trust).

In the case of a married couple, it is quite common for the contract owner to be one or both spouses and for the annuitant to be one or both spouses. This type of multiple titling is to protect the assets of the couple in the case of the untimely death of the annuitant. After all, if the annuitant were to die before the death of both spouses, most couples would not want the annuity proceeds to go to a charity or child while one or both spouses were still alive.

Single persons, widows, and widowers usually name themselves as the contract owner and annuitant, while listing a loved one or entity (for example, living trust, charity, or corporation) as the beneficiary. By making such an election, the individual retains complete control and dominion over the investment during his or her lifetime. Upon the death of the annuitant (a sole individual who is also the owner in this example), the money will automatically pass to the intended heir (for example, children, nephews, nieces, a charity, or trust). The contract owner can change the beneficiary or beneficiaries at any time; consent by the existing beneficiaries is not necessary.

Now that you know the players (the insurer, the contract owner, the annuitant, and the beneficiary), let us look at the two different types of fixed-rate annuities.

Types of Annuities: Immediate or Deferred

There are two ways to classify annuities:

1. How soon you start receiving income.
2. How the money is invested.

When the insurance company starts sending you checks depends on whether you choose an *immediate* annuity or *deferred* annuity. The investment decision is determined by either selecting a fixed-rate or variable annuity. You will first learn about the income aspect of annuities before moving on to the investment options.

If you purchase an immediate annuity, you are instructing the company to start sending you checks as soon as possible. Immediate annuities are designed for individuals or couples who want to rely on receiving a specific amount of money. The money may be the person or couple's sole source of income or merely to supplement other monies coming in. The check can be used for anything you want; after all, it is your money.

The checks can either be sent monthly, quarterly, or annually. The amount of each check does not fluctuate; the specific dollar amount of these checks, however, depends on how much you deposit with the insurance company, how many years of income you want, and the competitiveness of the insurer.

You should invest in an annuity as if you were purchasing a bank CD; hopefully, you will be doing some shopping before you make the commitment. When you invest in a CD, one of the things you are looking for is the highest rate of return. When shopping for an immediate annuity, part of your decision as to which company to use will depend upon how much money they are willing to send you each month. Thus, when you or your advisor compare annuities, one of the questions that should be asked is, "Okay, annuity XYZ, if I give you $10,000, how much will you send me each month for the rest of my life and/or the next five, 10, 20, 30, or more years?" Once the insurance company gives you a specific quote such as, "We will send you $374 each month for the next five years," have your advisor contact several other companies and find out what *they* will offer.

Like any other type of investment, product, or service, some companies are more competitive than others. It pays to do some homework and find out who will give you the best possible deal.

Some investors want income on a regular basis for a specific period of time. This period of time may range anywhere from just a few years to the lifetime of one or two people. Some annuities may offer handsome payments for a specific time, perhaps five years, but are not competitive if income for a lifetime is needed. Once you decide how long you want to receive an income stream, the task of comparing one company against another becomes much easier.

All other things being equal, the longer the time chosen, the less income you will receive per period (month, quarter, or year). Therefore, someone who has $50,000 and wants an immediate annuity structured for monthly payments for a 10-year period will get larger monthly checks than someone who has the same amount of money to invest, but is looking for monthly income for life (assuming her or his life expectancy is greater than 10 years).

Most people who purchase an annuity want their money to grow. These same people may or may not ever need an income stream. They are attracted to deferred annuities because this type of annuity provides them with the flexibility of having growth for a short or long period of time. Also, if they want, they can receive income from the annuity either through sporadic or scheduled withdrawals.

Investors purchase bank CDs because they want the interest income or because they plan on "rolling over" the CD and the interest upon maturity into another CD. Deferred annuities can be structured in a similar fashion. Annuity owners can request that a certain amount of income be sent to them annually.

In the alternative, part or all of the principal can also be sent out at anytime. Depending on several different conditions (discussed in the next chapter), the redemption of part or all of one's investment may or may not be subject to penalties, taxes, or both. However, in most cases, the owner of the annuity simply has the principal and any earned interest, growth, or both automatically reinvested, similar to someone who invests in a money market fund. When you invest in a money market fund, your account grows each day; the next day your principal and interest, or growth, is also compounding.

Deferred annuities can offer a great deal of flexibility. Anything earned in the account can be automatically reinvested, thereby providing an even greater return, or taken out. The contract owner also has the ability, subject to possible costs, to terminate the investment or simply withdraw part of the principal.

Advantages of Annuities

Annuities, which have been around for over a hundred years, provide more features than virtually any other investment. These traits include safety of the industry, reserve requirements, financial clout, the use of outside rating services, tax-deferred growth, tax-free exchanges, performance, professional management, no commission charge to the client, withdrawal options, a guaranteed death benefit, and avoidance of probate.

Safety

No one has ever lost a dime in a fixed-rate annuity. The track record for safety of this conservative investment vehicle is unequaled.

When you purchase a fixed-rate annuity, your principal is guaranteed every day. You can terminate the contract after being in it for only a day, month, year, or decade and always be assured that your contributions are intact. There are very few investments that can use the phrase "principal guaranteed at all times." In fact, the *only* other types of investments that can legitimately make this claim are accounts up to $100,000 at financial institutions insured by FDIC, and certain types of insurance contracts.

US government securities, such as T-bills and T-bonds, are only guaranteed as to face value if they are held until maturity. It is very likely that you can purchase a T-bill today and sell it tomorrow or next week for less than you paid for it. In the case of long-term securities, such as government bonds that mature in 20 to 30 years, they can literally lose half of their value or more within a few years if interest rates steadily increase. This occurred to bond buyers in the mid 1970's who sold their long-term obligations during the very early 1980's. It should be quickly pointed out, however, that if you hold a government security until its *maturity*, face value and interest are guaranteed.

Not only is your principal in a fixed-rate annuity guaranteed *at all times*, the *interest rate* received or credited to your account is also guaranteed for a specific period of time. Depending on the contract you choose, the locked-in rate of return may be for one, three, five, or more years.

Notice that this section on safety deals only with fixed-rate annuities. The value of a variable annuity can fluctuate daily. Principal is not guaranteed on a day-to-day basis; it is secured through the guaranteed death benefit (see the next chapter). Furthermore, the rate of return in a variable annuity is not guaranteed either; the one exception being if one opts for the fixed-rate subaccount (similar to locking in a CD rate).

At first glance, you may wonder why fixed-rate annuities have such strong guarantees and variable annuities do not. Keep in mind that in a variable annuity, *you* decide which type of portfolios to go into and with what dollar amounts. And, just like mutual funds, real estate, individual stocks, or bonds, you have the potential for making, or losing, a modest or large amount of money.

Reserve Requirements

When you deposit a dollar in a bank account, the bank, by law, must keep a certain amount on reserve. The amount depends on the type of account, but ranges from three to 12 cents on the dollar.

When you purchase a fixed-rate annuity, the insurance company, by law, must set aside *over* a dollar in reserves. The insurer can only use these excess reserves to settle the withdrawals and redemptions of annuity owners. They cannot use the money to settle insurance claims, pay overhead, settle bad debts, or any other non-related annuity item.

The question often arises as to *where* the insurer gets the excess monies to supplement annuity deposits for reserve purposes. The answer is from other profit centers. Conceptually, annuity business represents, by far, the smallest source of revenue for the insurance industry. Insurers generally derive much more income from selling life and other forms of insurance.

Financial Clout

There are over 2,000 different life insurance companies in the United States. Collectively, these companies own, control, or manage more assets than *all of the banks in the world combined.* The insurance industry of North America owns, controls, or manages more assets than *all of the oil companies in the world combined.*

During the Great Depression, it was not the government that bailed out the banking industry, it was our insurance companies. If there were ever a financial collapse in this nation, the insurance industry would be the second to the last entity to fold—second only to the government. And this "second billing" is only true because the government has taxing power and, of course, the ability to print money.

If the insurance industry were to ever collapse, we would fondly look back at the Great Depression as a *walk in the park* in comparison.

State Legal Reserve Pools

Most states require that any insurer doing business in the state must become part of the legal reserve pool. This pool protects annuity investors and others who purchase life insurance products or policies.

The reserve pool operates in a straightforward manner. If an insurance company goes out of business, the remaining insurers must assume the liabilities and obligations of the now defunct insurer. The liability assumed by any one insurance company depends on how much business it does in that particular state. If insurance company LMN sells 2% of all insurance and annuities issued in that state, then LMN must accept 2% of any bankrupt insurer's obligations.

If your state has a legal reserve system, it may be useful to see how it works. The system and its extent of coverage can vary from state to state. Nevertheless, if an insurance company wishes to do business in a state that has such a reserve, it must join the pool. Insurers who do not join such systems will be banned from the state by the insurance commissioner.

Rating Services

Even though annuities have a perfect track record, some companies are safer than others. During the last few years, we have read about some insurers' troubled portfolios that contain large amounts of junk bonds and poor real estate holdings. And, even though no one has ever lost a dime in a fixed-rate annuity, these relatively new developments have caused some alarm. It is for this reason that more and more people are concerned about the quality of their insurance company.

The A.M. Best Company is a neutral, unbiased source, that rates insurance companies as to their current financial soundness and ability to pay future insurance and annuity claims. A.M. Best Co., an Oldwick, New Jersey company has been in the business since 1899. Their job is somewhat similar to Moody's and Standard

& Poor's, two well-known stock and bond rating services.

The highest rating an insurance company can receive is A+ (superior); the second highest rating is A (excellent). Most investors should stick with companies that have an A or A+ rating. There are several dozen companies that have one of these two ratings. Equally important, you do not give up anything by using a highly rated company.

Some investors like junk (high-yield) bonds because of their perceived higher return. It is viewed as a tradeoff, higher risk for the chance of getting a higher yield. Fortunately, this is not the case with lower-rated insurance companies and products. The investor gets very little, if any, extra return by buying a fixed-rate annuity from a lesser-rated company.

During the past few years, savvy insurance advisors have begun to look for a second rating. These advisors will only recommend annuities and insurance products to their clients if the insurer has a top rating from A.M. Best and either Moody's or Standard & Poor's.

If you are investing in a variable annuity, the rating of the insurance company is usually of little importance. The reason for this somewhat lack of concern is because when you invest in a variable annuity, your fate is not tied to the solvency of the insurer; you are not investing in the assets of the insurance company. Money invested in a variable annuity is automatically turned over to the different portfolio managers of the subaccounts. It is the performance of your subaccounts that determine the safety and return on your investment. These portfolio managers are not buying securities issued by the insurer.

Despite what has just been discussed, most variable annuity owners still like the idea of dealing with a highly rated company. Fortunately, potential performance or investment flexibility does not suffer by opting for a safe annuity issuer.

Tax-Deferred Growth

One of the chief reasons why tens of millions of people around the world are attracted to annuities is because money in an annuity grows and compounds tax-deferred. There is nowhere on your tax return to indicate the value, interest, yield, or growth of your fixed-rate or variable annuity.

The only time you pay taxes on your annuity is if you withdraw growth or interest from the account. For example, if someone invested $20,000 in a fixed or variable annuity and the contract was now worth $55,000, the first $35,000 taken out would be taxable; the remaining $20,000 would not be taxed since this is considered a return of principal and the IRS never taxes return of principal.

The interest or growth is taxable in the year in which it is withdrawn and only on the amount actually received. Continuing the example from above, if the insurer withdrew $6,000 from the annuity that had grown from $20,000 to $55,000, only the $6,000 would be taxed. Subsequent redemptions would be taxed in the year of distribution; the final $20,000, in this example, would not be taxed, since that represents your original principal. As a side note, you cannot claim that the first money withdrawn was contributed dollars and therefore not taxable. The IRS no longer allows this option for contracts purchased after 1981.

Participants in annuities purchased before 1981 can opt to withdraw principal first and growth, interest, or both later. By using such a strategy, no taxes would be paid on any of the redemptions until such cumulative withdrawals equaled the contract owner's contributions (principal).

With a fixed-rate annuity, you can avoid income taxes indefinitely. The death of the annuitant would normally mean that the contract is terminated. However, if one spouse is named as the annuitant and the other spouse is named as the beneficiary, the contract can continue. The surviving spouse has the option of either liquidating part or all of the investment without cost, fee, or penalty by either the IRS or the issuer (the insurance company). Withdrawals or complete liquidations could trigger an *income tax* event to the extent that any monies received by the survivor were considered growth or interest.

The surviving spouse does not have to terminate the contract upon the death of the other spouse in this example. The remaining spouse can take over the investment and postpone any income tax event. The contract would then continue until the death of the surviving spouse. If the remaining spouse later remarries and names the "new" spouse as the beneficiary the tax deferral could last until the death of both of these spouses.

Sooner or later, all spouses will die. Upon the death of the final spouse, the non-spousal beneficiaries are entitled to the proceeds. These beneficiaries have four choices:

1. Pay taxes immediately.
2. Make withdrawals during the next five years, paying taxes along the way.
3. Wait up to five years, make a complete liquidation, and then pay taxes.
4. Annuitize (a concept that is discussed later) and pay some taxes with each withdrawal.

Each of these four options are discussed following by use of the same example.

Suppose that Mary and John Smith bought an annuity in 1980 for $40,000. John dies in 1989 and Mary dies in 1991; the children inherit an annuity that is now worth $100,000. The beneficiaries could withdraw the entire $100,000 and pay income taxes on the $60,000 gain. A taxable event would occur in the calendar year in which the $60,000 was received.

The children, or whoever the beneficiaries are, do not have to take the proceeds from the annuity upon death of the final spouse. They may make withdrawals systematically or sporadically during the next five years. They can take odd or similar amounts at any time. Any amount withdrawn would be taxed in the year in which it was received. If the children took out $15,000 in 1993, then taxes would be due on $15,000 worth of "income" received for the 1993 calendar year. If $10,000 more was taken out in 1994, taxes would be due on that amount for the 1994 calendar year. If this option is used, the only IRS requirement is that the contract must be completely liquidated within five years after the death of the final spouse. In our example of $40,000 growing to $100,000, the final $40,000 withdrawn would not be taxed, since it is still considered a return of principal.

The third option is to let the $100,000 contract continue to grow and compound tax-deferred for up to five years. At the end of five years, suppose that the contract is worth $165,000. The beneficiaries would be required to liquidate the entire investment and pay taxes on the difference between the amount withdrawn and principal ($165,000–$40,000=taxes due on $125,000 gain). Remember, the beneficiaries do not have to wait five years to make a complete liquidation. The entire amount can be withdrawn at anytime during this five-year period.

The fourth option is *annuitization*. Annuitization simply means that the beneficiary will receive a specific amount each month until their share, plus any accumulating interest or growth, has been completely withdrawn. These withdrawals have a certain tax benefit because the IRS considers each check a partial return of principal and therefore not taxable. This concept is discussed in "The Annuitant" section, earlier in this chapter.

Tax-Free Exchanges

Sometimes you go into one investment and later discover that it is not what you wanted or its quality has changed. One of the advantages of annuities is that you can change companies for whatever reason you like. You simply have your money moved from one annuity to another.

This move is known as a *1035 exchange* and is named after the Internal Revenue Code (IRC) section that allows such exchanges. These moves are also known as *tax-free exchanges*, since you do not pay any taxes. Always keep in mind that the only time you pay taxes on the growth or interest in an annuity is when you make withdrawals or a complete liquidation.

In order for you to take advantage of a tax-free exchange, the money from one insurer must go directly to another insurance company. You cannot have the check sent to you first. The IRS allows such 1035 exchanges because the money is never seen or touched by anyone except the insurers.

Tax-free exchanges are easy to do. You simply find a new annuity (company) where you want to move the contract, and fill out their application along with a separate form identified as a *1035 Exchange Request.* You then send in these two forms, along with your existing contract to the new company. The new insurer takes care of the rest. If you cannot find your existing contract, which is usually a few dozen pages in length, you simply fill out a *Lost Contract Form* and send it to the company where you want to transfer your assets.

Exchanges are simple and easy. You do not have to contact the person who sold you the original annuity. The Lost Contract Form and 1035 Exchange Request are each less than a page in length. You can make a tax-free exchange at any time. You are not limited by number or exchanges per year.

Although 1035 exchanges are straightforward and do not trigger an IRS penalty or tax, they may include a penalty by the insurance company. Whether an insurance company penalty will occur depends on the specifics of the contract. Normally, no penalties occur if the money has stayed with the original issuer for a certain number of years. With some companies, this period of time is as little as one year; however, most insurers have a penalty schedule that lasts for five to seven years. A few policies have a penalty that never completely disappears.

No Commission Charge

Whether you invest in a fixed-rate or variable annuity, 100% of your money goes to work for you from day one. You pay no commission when you go into an annuity. Furthermore, you do not pay a commission when you withdraw part of the account or liquidate the entire contract. A few companies still charge an initial "load" or commission, but this is certainly the exception and not the rule.

The broker or advisor you deal with gets paid a commission from the insurance company. Bypassing your stockbroker, insurance agent, or financial planner does not benefit you in the least. The insurance company will either keep the commission or pay it out to one of their producers. It should not make any difference to you anyway; all of your money is being invested.

Since the insurance company (annuity issuer) pays the commission, it is in your best interest that you make sure that someone who can later help out receives the fee. By ensuring that your agent or advisor receives the fee, she or he should be obligated to answer any questions or facilitate any changes you might have now or in the future. This broker can also research other companies if your annuity somehow becomes shaky or fails to perform as expected.

Annuities are referred to as *no load* or *commission free*, since any commission paid comes directly our of the insurance company's pocket. The commission normally ranges from one to six percent; the exact amount depends upon the *type* of annuity and the penalty period. The most common rate paid by an annuity company is four percent.

Sending your money directly into the insurance company will not save you anything. A much better strategy is to make sure that your representative, whether he or she works at a bank, savings and loan, brokerage firm, insurance agency, or financial planning group, knows that you are going through them and that you expect quality service and advice in the future.

Withdrawal Options

The good news is that you can always take out part or all of your money at anytime from a fixed-rate or variable annuity. The bad news is that the withdrawal *may* be subject to a penalty.

Most annuities allow withdrawals of up to 10% per year without cost, fee, or penalty. The free withdrawal is usually based on a percentage of your principal, not the current value. Thus, if Sven Haynie initially invests $20,000 in an annuity and later adds $30,000, he can withdraw $5,000 each year, *after the first year*, without any cost. This is true even if his account has a current value of $90,000. Some companies calculate the free withdrawal based upon *the greater of* current value or principal contributions. In such a case, Sven could withdraw $9,000 (10% of $90,000).

A few companies allow withdrawals of up to 15% per year. Whatever rate your company allows, keep in mind two points:

1. Close to 75% of all people who invest in an annuity never take any money out.
2. The restrictions on withdrawals eventually disappear.

The restrictions referred to in number two mean that you can take out more than 10% per year, but you will pay a penalty. The amount of penalty depends on the type of contract you have and the insurance company you use. The penalty cannot eat into your principal (unlike the penalties found in a CD). Some companies let you take out all of your interest or growth each year, penalty free. Other annuities impose a penalty for excess withdrawals during the first five, six, seven, or eight years. A small number of companies impose a penalty on "excess" withdrawals at anytime during the life of the contract. Penalties are discussed in the next chapter. For recap purposes, the following example may be helpful.

Suppose that you invested $500,000 in the GHI annuity and the account was currently worth $800,000. As with most companies, GHI allows free annual withdrawals of up to 10%, based on the value of original contributions. In this case you could take out $50,000 each year without penalty during the penalty period. At the end of five years, you could withdraw as much as you wanted from GHI without cost. But, suppose during the first few years of the investment you needed $70,000 quickly.

GHI would allow you to take out $50,000 during that year without cost. The remaining $20,000 you needed would be subject to a penalty. If this request was made during the second year of the investment, the penalty would probably be in the five percent range. The penalty is imposed only on the excess amount; the amount above the free withdrawal. In this example, five percent, or $1,000 would be charged (5% of $20,000). The investor would end up getting $69,000 of the $70,000 requested.

Who Should Buy Fixed-Rate Annuities?

Usually when you invest in a fixed-rate annuity, the longer you are willing to commit your money, the higher the interest rate you will receive. The interest you are credited can either be sent to you annually or reinvested so that you have a larger amount earning interest, a concept known as *compound interest* (interest earning interest).

Fixed-rate annuities are most popular with people who want assurances as to the safety of their principal. These people also want to know exactly what they can expect in the way of interest on their money. Fixed-rate annuities, since they provide guarantees as to principal and rate of return, are ideal investment candidates for conservative investors or anyone who wants to know exactly what he or she will have at the end of a specific period of time.

These types of annuities are not just for the timid or cautious. Fixed-rate annuities can provide a great stabilizing force for moderate or aggressive investors who need some balance in their overall portfolio. No matter what happens to real estate, stocks, bonds, gold, or mutual funds, all investors in fixed-rate annuities know that at least one part of their holdings is safe, secure, and *guaranteed.*

As you can see, in an uncertain tax and economic environment, fixed-rate annuities offer some tremendous guarantees and benefits not found with other investments. The next chapter describes variable annuities. Variable and fixed-rate annuities share many of the same features but, as you will see, variable annuities offer investment alternatives not found in fixed-rate contracts.

Summary

To make the deficit go down, the President and Congress will be looking for ways to minimize the federal burden. Through legislation, employers will be required to pick up more of the tab in the area of health care, unemployment, and retirement. These companies, in turn, will be looking to its employees to pay a greater share of what used to be partially or fully paid by the employer. This means that during the next several years, the percentage or amount of money contributed for your retirement by your boss will be lower. Many plans will be eliminated altogether, saving your company large sums of money, but leaving you possibly out in the cold when it comes to retirement benefits.

One of the best ways for you to counter such a scale-down at work, is by taking matters in your own hands and investing in a fixed-rate annuity. You will not receive any deductions for your investment (contributions), but you will enjoy the same tax-deferred growth as a pension or profit-sharing plan. When you eventually decide to take money out of your annuity, you are not required to do so the year after you reach 70½ (like you are with traditional retirement plans). Moreover, when you make withdrawals, you are not taxed on the dollars you contributed (unlike a qualified retirement plan).

Fixed-rate annuities are something you should consider if you are looking for a conservative place to investment your money. This investment vehicle has a tremendous advantage over bank CDs, government obligations, and traditional money market funds, which are all taxable. The benefits of tax-deferred growth over a fully taxable investment become more dramatic the longer the holding period.

Middle and upper-income people who receive social security benefits are faced with the reality that a greater percentage of such benefits will be taxed in the future. The formula used to determine how much of these benefits are subject to tax includes income you receive from all sources, plus the interest from tax-free bonds. The accumulated growth (or interest) in an annuity is not used in such computation; one more reason you should be looking at fixed-rate or variable annuities.

10

Variable Annuities

There will be a lot of things going on during this new presidential leadership. Whether you are the type of investor who wants to seize the moment or one who waits patiently for some type of trend to develop, variable annuities are an investment vehicle you should seriously consider. Ever since Carter became president, there have been significant changes to the Tax Code with every changing of the guard. One of the few areas that has, and will, remain intact is fixed-rate and variable annuities.

A variable annuity works like a mutual fund family with three important differences:

1. Your investments in a variable annuity grow and compound tax-deferred.
2. Variable annuities provide a guaranteed death benefit.
3. With most variable annuities you never pay a commission.

In a variable annuity, your contributions are segregated and *you* decide how your money is to be invested. *Segregation* means that your investment is not at risk even if the insurer goes bankrupt. Most insurers do not even keep your investment; it is immediately transferred to the money-management company, usually a mutual fund group. You can choose among stock, bond, government obligation, gold, and money market accounts, just like you would choose among different types of mutual funds.

Variable annuities were first introduced in this country in the early 1950's. One of the best known and oldest variable annuities is the College Retirement and Equities Fund (CREF). At the end of 1991, it was estimated that there was over $200 billion in variable annuities and well over eight million contract owners.

As the name implies, variable annuities offer the investor a variety of options. Let us see how these different investment options have fared against mutual funds in similar categories as well as well-known benchmark indices.

Track Record: Aggressive Growth (Small Cap) Accounts

This following table shows how the entire aggressive growth category of variable annuities has performed against the S & P 500 over the past one, three, five, and 10 years, ending December 31, 1992. The category small cap mutual funds is also shown for comparison purposes

	Years			
Category	1	3	5	10
Small Cap Accounts	12.1%	14.5%	16.9%	12.8%
S & P 500	8.4%	11.1%	16.2%	16.3%
Small Cap Mutual Funds	8.3%	12.7%	16.0%	9.7%

The reason that this category of variable annuities did not outperform the S & P over the past five and 10 years is because the 1980's favored large stocks. Nevertheless, notice how small cap variable annuities have performed similarly to small cap mutual funds over the past one, three, five, and 10 years.

Track Record: High-Yield Bond Accounts

The following table shows how the entire high-yield bond category has performed against high-quality corporate and high-yield mutual funds over the past one, three, five, and 10 years, ending December 31, 1992.

	Years			
Category	1	3	5	10
High-Yield Bond Accounts	15.6%	13%	9.8%	11.3%
High-Quality Bond Funds	6.5%	9.4%	9.5%	10.6%
High-Yield Bond Funds	17.7%	12.6%	9.4%	10.1%

Track Record: International Bond Accounts

The following table shows how the entire international bond category has performed against the Lehman Brothers Government/Corporate Bond Index and the Consumer Price Index (CPI) over the past one, five, and 10 years, ending December 31, 1992.

The Lehman Brothers index is the most commonly used way to measure the performance of domestic bond. This form of comparison is rough because global bonds only include modest amounts of US bonds. Nevertheless, investors will get a good sense as to how one type of bond has performed against another. The category World Bond Mutual Funds (US and international bonds) is also shown for comparison purposes.

	Years			
Category	1	3	5	10
International Bond Accounts	-4%	8.0%	7.4%	11.3%
Gov't./Corp. Bond Index	7.6%	10.6%	10.7%	11.5%
World Bond Mutual Funds	2.4%	9.3%	8.2%	12.7%

Track Record: Foreign (International) Stock Accounts

The following table shows how the entire international stock category has performed against the S & P 500 and the Morgan Stanley EAFE Index over the past one, three, five, and 10 years, ending December 31, 1992. The letters EAFE stand for Europe, Australia, and the Far East; this is a weighted index—Japan easily represents the largest component of this index. The EAFE index is the most widely used measurement of foreign stock markets. The category Foreign Stock Mutual Funds is also shown for comparison purposes

Category	Years 1	3	5	10
International Stock Accounts	–6.5%	–2.1%	4.3%	N/A
EAFE Index	–12.2%	–9.0%	1.3%	16.7%
Foreign Stock Mutual Funds	–4.8%	–1.9%	5.8%	13.2%

Monitoring Performance

One of the nice features of annuities is that you can always call them and find out how your investment is doing. Most annuity companies have toll-free telephone numbers. Several companies have an automated service that can give you information, including account balances, 24 hours a day, seven days a week.

In addition to contacting the insurance company, you can also monitor performance by subscribing to one of several periodicals. *Barron's*, a weekly publication, lists unit values of several hundred variable annuities each issue. *The Wall Street Journal* has also increased their coverage of annuities and periodically runs performance figures on some of the best and worst performing variable annuities.

For serious variable annuity investors, there are several professional monitoring services that you can subscribe to. One of the very best is *The VARDS Report*, a monthly publication. An annual subscription costs $698. It includes contract information for all products followed. VARDS is published by:

Financial Planning Resources, Inc.
P.O. Box 161998
Miami, Florida 33116

For a free sample copy, write or call:
(305) 252-4600.

Another source you may want to consider is published by Lipper Analytical Securities Corporation. The *Lipper Variable Insurance Products Performance Analysis Service* contains performance figures on variable life insurance as well as variable annuities. For a sample copy, write to

Lipper Analytical Services, Inc.
47 Maple St.
Summit, New Jersey 07901

(201) 273-2772.

Variable Annuity Features

As previously mentioned, variable and fixed-rate annuities share many of the same features such as tax-deferred growth, tax-free exchanges, no commission charge, withdrawal options, and the avoidance of probate. However, since there are differences between fixed and variable annuities, there are some guarantees that are unique to variable contracts. Specifically, with a variable annuity, you also get a guaranteed death benefit, professional management, and the potential for greater tax-deferred growth.

Before getting into each of these additional features, there are a couple of points that should be cleared up in favor of fixed-rate annuities. First, fixed-rate contracts do not need a guaranteed death benefit, since the account's value is guaranteed every day. Second, since fixed-rate annuities are very limited as to how your money is invested, the need for professional management is not as great. The people who invest fixed-rate monies are professionals who specialize in a narrow range of assets, including government obligations, corporate bonds, and mortgages. Finally, although variable annuities do have the potential for greater growth, they can also drop in value due to a bad stock or bond market. A fixed-rate annuity can never drop in value, since it is not subjected to such risks.

Having examined these things, let us now explore these additional features in greater detail.

Guaranteed Death Benefit

Previous discussion has pointed out that your principal is *guaranteed* every day in a fixed-rate annuity. A guaranteed death benefit is of no use for an investment that carries such an assurance. That is why this section deals with *variable* annuities only.

When you invest in a variable annuity, it automatically contains a guaranteed death benefit. The guarantee works as follows: Upon the death of the annuitant, the beneficiary will receive the *greater of* the principal, plus any ongoing additions, or the value of the account as of the annuitant's date of death.

This guaranteed death benefit makes the variable annuity an ideal investment for an older couple that wants a high income stream or growth to offset inflation. One spouse can name herself or himself as the annuitant, invest in one or more of the stock or bond subaccounts, knowing that upon their death, the survivor will get back the greater of the amount invested or current value.

As an example, suppose that Mr. and Mrs. Pete Ward invest $400,000 in a variable annuity, and Mr. Ward names himself as the annuitant. He also feels lucky and decides to put the entire $400,000 in the aggressive stock portfolio. A few months or years later, there is a stock-market crash, recession, depression, or other terrible event. The account drops in value to $5,000; the Ward's have lost $395,000. But have they? Later, Mr. Ward is in an accident and dies. Mrs. Ward will receive $400,000 as the beneficiary, even though the account on Mr. Ward's death was worth approximately $5,000.

The guaranteed death benefit is based on the greater of all contributions (investments made by the owner) or value on the date of the annuitant's death, whichever is greater. Suppose in the above example, that during their lifetimes the $400,000 grew to $1,200,000, dropped to $50,000, went up to $900,000 and then dropped to $750,000 on the date of Mr. Ward's death. Mrs. Ward would be entitled to $750,000. She is not entitled to the peak value of the account during the annuitant's lifetime.

Finishing the example, if the Ward's originally invested $400,000 and then later added another $500,000, the minimum death benefit would be $900,000, reduced by any withdrawals made from the account. It would not be fair to the insurance company to reimburse you for money you had voluntarily taken out before the annuitant's death. The guaranteed death benefit lasts until you terminate the contract or annuitize the investment.

Tax-Deferred Growth Revisited

To fully appreciate the benefits of tax-deferred growth, look at the following two tables. They give a visual depiction of what happens when a you make a single $10,000 investment in a tax-deferred vehicle such as an annuity, versus what you make in an investment that has the same rate of return, but is subject to current income taxes. The tables show the different results, assuming six and 14 percent growth rates. In each of these two tables, a 5-, 10-, 15-, and 20-year time period are covered. Notice how dramatic the benefits of tax deferral are if a higher rate of return is assumed.

6% Interest Rate

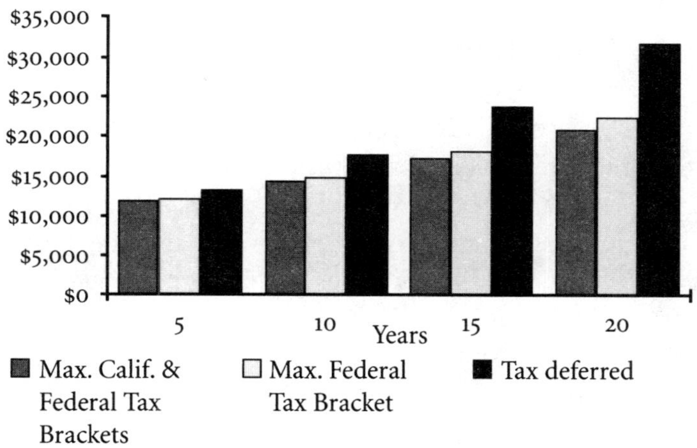

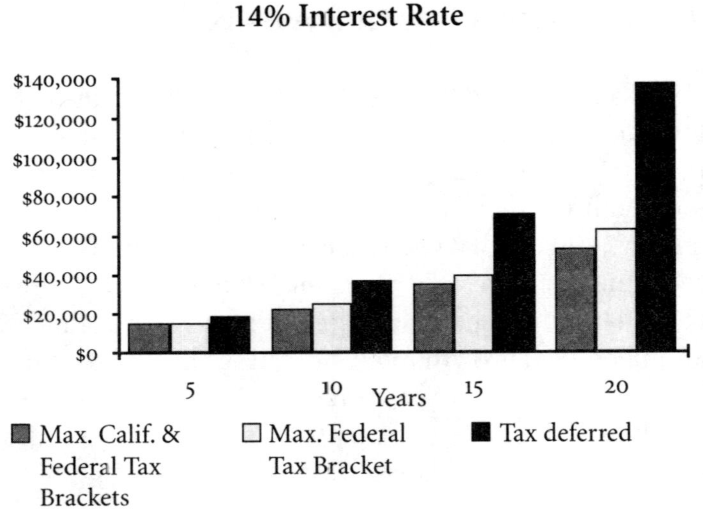

How Much Should You Invest in Annuities?

Annuities are the ideal choice for someone who is in a moderate or high tax bracket and is looking for a way to shelter current income or growth. *Fixed-rate* annuities are a smart alternative for CDs, money market accounts, GNMAs, Treasury bills, or other government obligations; particularly if you are the type of investor who only needs to touch such monies in the case of unforeseen circumstances. *Variable* annuities would be a proper choice for a taxpayer who is in a moderate or high tax bracket, and is tired of paying taxes on capital gains and dividends and interest from securities. They would also be a good substitution for mutual funds that exhibited high tax consequences.

As you can see, annuities can, and often should, play a major role in your investment plan. It is their flexibility and guarantees that make them an integral part of your financial security. As you or your advisor begin to look at different contracts, look for companies that have been in existence for several years, enjoy a strong reputation in the financial services community, and include the sub-accounts and provisions that are important to you.

The G.T. Global Allocator

With almost a quarter century of global investment experience and over $12 billion in assets under management, the G.T. Group is an acknowledged expert in global investing. In 1969, G.T. was founded on the premise that to effectively manage money globally they needed to maintain a *local presence* in key markets around the world—something not found with most money managers, mutual funds, or variable annuity groups.

The G.T. Global Allocator is a variable annuity contract issued by General American Life Insurance Company. Chartered in 1933, General American is a *Fortune 50* mutual life insurance company. General American has more than 30 years' experience in the annuity marketplace and currently has more than $2 billion in annuity assets. This is the first annuity program to offer investors *regional* stock funds, global bond funds, US stock and bond funds, and fixed-rate choices.

The variable annuity choices offered through the G.T. Global Allocator are managed by experienced professionals in London, San Francisco, Tokyo, Hong Kong, Sydney, and Singapore. These portfolio managers are well versed in local government policies and corporate customs. Their access to public and private leaders gives them the opportunity to identify and capitalize on investment trends as they develop.

The G.T. Variable Investment Funds include: a global growth and income fund, a US government bond fund, a global government bond fund, a money market fund, a US growth stock fund, and three regional stock funds (Pacific, Europe, and Latin America). Also offered are one-, three-, and six-year Guaranteed Interest Options.

For additional information call (800) 824-1580, or write to:

G.T. Global Financial Services
50 California Street, 27TH Floor
San Francisco, CA 94111

Summary

It is difficult to predict the next great investment opportunity. Will it be in metals, real estate, stocks, bonds, money market instruments, or foreign securities? Whatever it turns out to be, as a variable annuity investor, you can take advantage of this opportunity without selling one investment, triggering a tax event, and going into a new asset category. Variable annuities and variable life insurance (see the next chapter) are the only two ways you can take advantage of a changing climate under Clinton without paying taxes as you go along (unless you happen to have a qualified retirement plan that offers a wide range of investment choices).

Variable annuities offer all the benefits, features, and performance of mutual funds, but also offer features not found in funds, including

- Tax-deferred growth.
- Tax-advantaged income.
- A guaranteed death benefit.

Due to the pre-59½ IRS penalty, variable (as well as fixed-rate) annuities are best suited for investors who are at least in their mid-50's.

President Clinton is raising taxes on individuals and couples whose incomes are over a certain amount. Variable annuities are a way for you to participate in the domestic and foreign stock and bond markets without paying any taxes. This vehicle is the perfect hideout for those investors who are waiting for Clinton's successor. Regardless of whether a Democrat or Republican is in charge, the tax benefits and assurances of variable annuities make them an appropriate investment, *even if you're an Independent.*

11

Variable Life Insurance

YOUR FAMILY MAY BE ROBBED of the financial security you were planning if you die young. Even if you already have a large estate, it can be whittled down rather quickly if the family business, real estate, or securities must be sold in a depressed market to pay estate taxes. There is only one vehicle available that can protect your estate against such a disaster: life insurance. If you want the double benefit of protecting your family and benefiting yourself while you are alive, then read on. Most people dismiss life insurance because they feel that it is not something that can benefit them. These same people do not realize that if you buy the right type of insurance, everyone concerned can reap the benefits, even the person being insured.

Before detailing the benefits referred to above, let us review some basic concepts about life insurance. Once you understand how insurance works, understanding the benefits of variable life insurance will be much clearer. As you will see, this is yet another asset that you should consider in an uncertain economic, income tax, and estate tax environment. And there will be tremendous change under President Clinton.

Life insurance is something that every adult needs to *consider*, whether you are 18 or 80. This type of insurance is not something that everyone should have, but you need to examine its place in your retirement and estate planning. You may discover that you need more insurance, less insurance, a different type of policy, or possibly even no life insurance. There are multiple reasons why life insurance may be beneficial to you and your loved ones. Life insurance provides these three benefits:

1. A source of revenue to replace the earning capacity of someone now deceased.
2. An investment.
3. Greater flexibility in estate planning.

There are many reasons why people buy life insurance. The most common reason is to provide a source of ready cash for the named beneficiaries. Proceeds from a life insurance policy are received free from federal and state income taxes.

The death benefit can be used as a means to partially or fully offset the income of a breadwinner. Depending on the amount of coverage, income generated by investing the proceeds can last for the survivors' lives or until they are able to financially adjust for the loss. Some people want life insurance to pay off certain debts in the event of their death. The most common concern here is the home mortgage. The income earner wants to make sure that if he or she dies then their spouse, children, or both will at least be able to live in a home that is owned free and clear. Still others buy life insurance to settle potential business disputes in the event of the death of a key employee or owner. Referred to as *buy-sell agreements*, the amount of the death benefit is large enough to pay the deceased owner's family for the deceased's share of the business.

Some types of life insurance include a savings or investment portion, and can be viewed as a form of investing. Income earned in a life insurance policy is either tax-deferred or tax-free. These tax advantages are not generally found with other types of investments. This makes certain forms of whole life insurance (explained in detail later) a powerful retirement planning tool; the earnings can be used while the insured is still alive, as an emergency fund, or accumulated to possibly enhance the death benefit. Upon the death of the insured, the beneficiary receives the face amount of the policy free of any income taxes.

If you have an estate that is worth more than $600,000 ($1.2 million if you are married), you may also want to consider using life insurance as an estate-planning tool. The death benefit can be used to pay part or all of any estate taxes due upon the death of the insured. As will be explained later in this chapter, life insurance can be a way to pay Uncle Sam death taxes for only five or 10 cents on the dollar.

Life Insurance Basics

When properly explained, life insurance can be easy to understand. There are three parties to every life insurance policy and there are two basic types of life insurance coverage. The three parties to a policy are:

1. The owner.
2. The insured.
3. The beneficiary.

The *owner* is usually the person who buys the policy. This is the person that pays the insurance company what are known as *premiums*. These payments, or premiums, may be made monthly, quarterly, semi-annually, annually, or all at once. The frequency of the premiums depends upon the type of policy you choose and the payment schedule you select. Any persons or entities, such as corporations, living trusts, children, or a couple can be the owner.

The *insured* is a specific person. If this person dies while the policy is in force, meaning that the premiums are current, then the insurance company pays the face amount of the policy, also referred to as the *death benefit*. This benefit is paid to the beneficiary. Like the contract owner, the *beneficiary* can be an individual, couple or entity. Ownership and beneficiary designations can be changed at anytime. The insured can only be changed by purchasing a new policy.

Life insurance comes in one of two basic forms: term or whole life. *Term* insurance is coverage in its purest form. All of the premiums you pay go toward coverage; there is no cash buildup, no investment, and no borrowing privileges. The life of the policy is its term. If you die during the life of the policy, then your beneficiaries receive payment.

Whole life insurance is simply term insurance coupled with a savings plan. Whole life premiums are more expensive, since a portion of each dollar received by the insurance company is used to fund the investment side of the policy. The investment portion of the whole life policy is known as its *cash value*. Furthermore, the amount of each dollar that goes toward an investment that you can later tap into depends upon the type of whole life policy and the rate charged by your insurer for mortality, administrative, and other expenses. Therefore, although there are only two major types of insurance, whole and term, there are several different forms that each come in.

The following table shows market share, based on annualized premiums for the year to date through September 1992, according to the monthly survey of *Life Insurance Sales* in the United States.

Type of Insurance	Percentage of Market Share
Universal Life	22%
Variable Life	2%
Variable Universal Life	10%
Term	13%
Whole Life	53%

The rate of growth of the policy's cash value depends on how such monies are invested. With some whole life policies you choose the investment vehicles; other types of whole life policies offer no investment options and the investment portion of your premium depends on the success of the insurance company's portfolio. In the case of variable life insurance, a type of whole life, you have investment choices.

Variable Life Insurance

Variable life insurance is a way of getting life insurance while building up a nest egg from the growth of the cash value portion of the policy. Like an annuity, the investment side of the policy grows and compounds tax-deferred. Unlike an annuity, variable life insurance can be funded in a manner that provides you, your heirs, or both with tax-free income.

When you buy life insurance you pay what are known as *premiums.* If you pay your premiums over at least a five-year period (seven years in some cases), you satisfy certain IRS regulations. The easiest way to structure a variable life insurance policy for individuals and couples interested in current income is to make premium payments for exactly five years and then never make another contribution. If properly structured, you, the investor can take money out of a variable life insurance policy free of income taxes forever. These withdrawals are considered either a *return of principal* or *loans,* neither of which are taxed by the IRS. After your death, your beneficiaries will receive a death benefit that is also free from income taxes. If you follow a few simple rules, no one will ever have to pay taxes on these distributions while you are alive or after your death. The following example shows how it works with these figures:

Variable Life Insurance

Number of Payment Years:	5
Annual Premium Amount:	$20,000
Insurance Amount:	$374,100
Assumed Rate of Growth:	11%
Sex:	Male

Premium Payment	Year	Variable Account	Surrender Value	Death Benefit
$20,000	1	$19,600	$14,700	$374,100
$20,000	2	41,100	36,200	374,100
$20,000	3	64,800	60,000	374,100
$20,000	4	90,900	86,300	374,100
$20,000	5	119,700	115,400	374,100
0	6	130,700	126,600	374,100
0	7	142,800	138,900	374,100
0	8	156,000	152,400	374,100
0	9	170,700	168,200	374,100
0	10	186,700	186,700	374,100
0	15	296,000	296,000	374,100
0	20	474,900	474,900	550,900
0	25	762,200	762,200	815,600
0	30	1,226,600	1,226,600	1,288,000
0	35	1,964,600	1,964,600	2,062,900
0	40	3,123,100	3,123,100	3,279,300
0	Age 95	4,978,400	4,978,400	5,028,200

As you review this illustration, keep in mind three things:

1. Annual contributions of $20,000 are being made only for each of the first five years.
2. The value of the variable account and the surrender value are not equal until the 10th year, meaning that there is an insurance company penalty if the policy is canceled during the first 10 years.
3. The variable account and surrender value figures could be much higher or lower than those shown, depending on the actual rate of return.

Due to the high initial costs, a variable life insurance program performs best if it is viewed as a long-term investment. Although the table above does not show this, it takes several years for the cash to build up in this account before you can make substantial *tax-free withdrawals.* To gain a better understanding about this point, ask your accountant or insurance advisor to explain the *7 Pay Test* to you as it relates to borrowing money out of an insurance policy.

Summary

Variable life insurance goes two steps beyond variable annuities:

1. There are life insurance proceeds.
2. You can receive money, during and after the insured's death, tax-free (versus tax-deferred with annuities).

The tax benefits that are afforded to life insurance policies, whether they are estate or income tax, whether you own term, traditional whole life, or variable life, will not disappear under this administration.

12

How to Title Your Accounts

WHAT DOES TITLING an account or asset have anything to do with investment strategies under Clinton and Gore? Well, even though President Clinton has not proposed legislation about titling accounts over the next 4–8 years, the information that follows will help you steer clear of disaster for you or your intended heirs under *any* presidential administration. It is fair to say that the return or safety of an investment is of little concern if you or your future beneficiaries cannot enjoy such rewards.

Learning about how to title ownership to your assets is the perfect transition between investing and financial (as well as estate) planning. In fact, prior to making an investment, you should know how you want to hold title, and how the account should read at the bank, brokerage firm, or county recorder's office.

How you own real estate and personal property can cost or save you thousands of dollars; for some people, tens of thousands of dollars. It may even cost you the property itself. There are important legal and tax consequences associated with every form of ownership. This chapter will show you all of the different ways you can own something. It discusses the advantages and disadvantages of each. After you finish reading this chapter, most of you will want to change the title to one or more of your holdings. As you will see, the changing of a title is simple, quick, and usually free. In the case of real estate, your county recorder's office will charge a fee in the neighborhood of $20 for such a transfer.

Titled property includes real estate, automobiles, mobile homes, boats, bank accounts, mutual funds, individual securities, and brokerage firm accounts. Title to these assets can be in held in one of the following manners:

- Separate
- Tenancy in common
- Joint tenancy with rights of survivorship
- Community property
- Tenancy by the entirety
- Custodian
- Partnership
- Corporation
- In trust

You cannot hold title to the same asset in different ways; you must choose only one. Each of these forms of ownership are described as follows.

Separate

Separate property includes all of those things you acquire while single. It consists of those items earned or acquired after legal separation or divorce. It also includes those things that you receive by gift or inheritance during marriage. Separate property maintains its identity unless it is transferred by the owner to some form of joint ownership or gifted to another person.

As the sole owner of separate property, only you can decide if and when the asset is to be sold or given to someone else. No other person, including your spouse, can transfer, buy, sell, or give away any of your separate property unless you give them permission.

Since only one name appears on the title, it is easy to transfer, sell, or refinance real estate or personal property. The owner simply signs his or her name to the document.

Tenancy in Common

Tenancy in common is a form of joint or co-ownership. As a *co-tenant,* you own the asset with one or more other people or entities (a corporation, trust, or partnership). You can sell, transfer, gift, or bequeath (leave in your will or trust) your interest to anyone, without the permission of the other co-owners. If the entire asset is being disposed of, all of the people listed on the title must approve and sign an agreement.

Joint Tenancy with Rights of Survivorship

The most common form of co-ownership is joint tenancy with rights of survivorship, often abbreviated as *jtwros.* Like tenancy in common, jtwros means that two or more individuals or entities own the asset and any co-owner is free to dispose of their share in any manner while they are alive. And, just like tenancy in common, all those shown on the title as owner must sign their names before the item can be transferred. However, unlike any other form of ownership, upon the death of one of the co-owners under jtwros, the decedent's share automatically passes on to the surviving tenants. Joint tenancy takes precedence over any will or trust. Therefore, even if you try to give jtwros property to someone else in your will, it will have no effect.

People own assets as joint tenants for one of three reasons:

1. Their real estate broker or title company either suggested or pointed out that most people take ownership in this form.
2. They want to avoid probate.
3. They are ignorant about this subject.

As you will see, there are numerous problems with joint tenancy.

Most married couples own property in joint tenancy. When the first spouse dies, the surviving spouse inherits the property outright. The decedent's name is taken off the title as soon as the survivor re-titles the property. Re-titling requires a certified copy of the death certificate and a letter of instruction from the survivor. This often only *postpones* probate. Unless the surviving spouse later adds a new joint tenant (for example, a child, friend, or new spouse), the asset may be subject to probate.

Adding another person to the title is common. However, this creates other problems. First, this new partner automatically inherits the property when the second spouse dies, regardless of what a will or trust might say to the contrary. You can list as many co-tenants as you want, but each of them will now be co-owners. The property cannot be transferred unless all sign the conveyance. If you have children who move around or are married to troublesome or greedy in-laws, getting everyone to sign may be difficult. Multiple ownership, however, poses a far greater problem.

Since a joint tenant is an owner, the property is subject to the claims of creditors and lawsuits. Whether the co-owner is your child, friend or other relative, if they are successfully sued, there may be a forced sale or lien on the asset. The suit may later be settled or won and the asset still sold to pay for legal expenses; it is very rare for the defendant or plaintiff to ever recover legal expenses, no matter how right they were. Listing anyone as a joint tenant who drives a car, is a professional, or owns a business greatly increases the odds that the asset may be lost. The chances of such an occurrence are even greater if the co-tenant is married. You would also have to be concerned about that spouse being subjected to a lawsuit.

Another problem with joint tenancy has to do with protecting your beneficiaries. If you are married and have children from a previous marriage, a joint tenancy with your spouse means that he or she gets the property when you die. This surviving spouse has no duty or obligation to later pass it on to *your* children. If the survivor has children of their own or later remarries, there is a good chance that the ultimate heir will be someone you may not have even met.

With rising health-care costs and people living longer, you may be hospitalized for an extended period or kept alive. If this situation arises and you can no longer sign your name due to a physical or mental impairment, then it may be difficult for your loved ones to raise needed cash to survive or pay your bills. More importantly, with the exception of your personal residence, these assets will have to be disposed of before there is any financial assistance from the state or federal government.

Joint tenancy increases the chances of a conservatorship. If any co-owner becomes incapacitated, a conservatorship must be established. A conservatorship involves time, money, lawyers, and the courts.

Up to now, all of the negative things associated with

joint tenancy are from events and circumstances that may or may not arise. But the worst part about joint tenancy is a certainty. This has to do with the sale or gifting of the asset.

Anytime a sale, transfer, gift, or inheritance of an asset is contemplated, always consider any potential income, gift, or estate tax. When you acquire an asset, such as a home, business interest, stock, or bond, you take on what is known as a *cost basis.* This basis is important if the asset is ever disposed of; any and all profits or losses are determined based on the asset's basis. The cost, or basis, is the purchase price minus any depreciation or plus any additions (such as fix-up expenses or additional contributions).

When personal property (such as stocks, bonds, cars, boats, jewelry, or furniture) or real estate is sold for more than the purchase price, a taxable event can occur. The profit, referred to as *gain,* is determined by subtracting the purchase price (adjusted for any depreciation or fix-up costs claimed) from the *net* sales price (the selling price minus any costs, fees or commissions). As an example, if you paid $20,000 for a car, spent $5,000 fixing it up, depreciated $6,000 of it as a business expense and then paid someone $1,000 to sell it for you for $22,000, the tax consequences would look like this:

	$20,000	Purchase Price
+	5,000	Fix-Up Costs
–	6,000	Depreciation
=	19,000	Adjusted–Cost Basis
–	22,000	Selling Price
=	3,000	Gross Profit
–	1,000	Selling Commission
=	2,000	Net (Taxable) Profit

This net figure results in a taxable event unless the final figure is zero or a negative number or the asset being sold is somehow sheltered (within a retirement plan, part of an annuity or a tax-free exchange). One of the goals of estate and financial planning is to lower, eliminate, or defer, whenever possible, any tax event. Such planning will be explored toward the end of the book.

Unless somehow sheltered, assets sold while you are *alive* are fully taxable if a net profit results. Assets sold for a loss may result in a tax loss that can be used to offset gains. You can also use a tax loss to offset earned income such as your salary. Death of an owner or co-owner can change the tax consequences due to what is known as a *step-up in basis.*

Stepped-Up Basis

A stepped-up basis means that, in the eyes of the IRS, the asset being sold or transferred now costs more than it originally did. This means that any resulting profit will be reduced or eliminated. A step-up in basis occurs only upon the death of a sole owner or co-tenant in the case of community property or joint tenancy with rights of survivorship. The best way to show how a new basis is calculated is by example.

Suppose that you were the *sole owner* of some stocks, bonds, personal property, or real estate that originally cost you $100,000. For the sake of illustration, assume that the cost basis is not altered because of any depreciation, additional contributions, or fix-up costs. The asset is now worth $300,000 and you decide to sell it. If the asset was sold for $300,000 you would have a $200,000 profit. Unless somehow sheltered, taxes on the $200,000 gain would be due for the year in which the asset was sold.

Change the set of facts slightly and assume that just before the sale occurred, you died. Your heirs would receive a step-up in basis equal to the fair market value of the asset as of the date of your death ($300,000 in this example). If the heirs later sold the asset, any profit or loss would be determined based on the new cost basis. If, in our example, the property you paid $100,000 for was worth $300,000 at your death and the heirs later sold it for $300,000, there would be no taxable gain. This is because the new basis is $300,000; your heirs received a 100% step-up in basis. This is one of the few ways in which income taxes can be avoided, but death must occur to get this tax advantage.

Let us change the facts again. Now assume that you and someone else own the property as joint tenants with rights of survivorship (jtwros). If a sale occurred *while both of you were alive* there would be a taxable gain of $200,000, just like what happened if you owned the asset as separate property. If, however, either tenant died before the sale, there would be an adjustment in the cost basis of the decendent's share. *Half* of the property would get a step-up in basis equal to *that share's* value at the date of death.

In our example, upon the death of a joint owner, his or her share is now considered to have an original purchase price of $150,000 (½ the fair market value at death), even though they only paid $50,000 for that interest. Any profit or loss is now based on the new cost basis. In this case, the new cost basis is the decendent's share, adjusted upward to $150,000. The surviving tenant's original cost, $50,000, or other half of the original purchase price, does not change. Taxes are based on an *adjusted basis* of $200,000 (the decendent's stepped-up half, $150,000, plus the survivor's half, $50,000). If the property were sold for $300,000, the surviving tenant would pay taxes on a gain of $100,000 (unless there was some exclusion, tax-free exchange, or the sold asset was part of a qualified retirement plan or annuity).

Let us change the facts one last time. Assume everything is the same, except this couple is married, they live in a community-property state, and the asset is titled as community property (for example, "Nathan and Ina Baty, c/p"). Upon the death of either spouse, the property will receive a 100% step-up in basis *on both halves*, even though only one spouse has died. If the property had been sold while both spouses were alive, there would have been a potential taxable gain of $200,000 (the $300,000 sales price minus the $100,000 purchase price). However, in this particular example, wherein one or both spouses have died, there is no taxable event, since the property has a new cost basis of $300,000. Any profit or loss is based on the new basis, $300,000, being subtracted from the sales price. In our example where the sales price is assumed to also be $300,000, there are no taxes due, since $300,000 minus $300,000 results in a gain of zero. Community property is discussed in the next section.

Keep in mind the following three points concerning community property and a step-up in basis:

1. The property must be titled as *community property prior to* the sale and death of either spouse.
2. Living in a community property state is not enough.
3. Death must occur to receive the stepped-up basis. This 100% step-up in basis also occurs if both spouses die at the same time.

All items titled as community property will receive a 100% step-up in basis upon the death of either the husband or wife, even if such items have been re-titled under the name of the trust.

Most people in community-property states take title to their home, savings accounts, and securities as jtwros with their spouse. As you can now see, this may be the biggest mistake they have ever made. Fortunately, you can go out and re-title the asset tomorrow for little or no cost. You do not need a lawyer or court order to make such a change. Simply contact the savings institution, brokerage firm or county recorders office and find out what form they require.

Community Property

There are seven community property states:

- Arizona
- California
- Idaho
- Nevada
- New Mexico
- Texas
- Washington

All other states, except Louisiana and the District of Columbia, are classified as *common-law* or *separate-property* states. Wisconsin is a common-law state, but has adopted marital property laws that are similar to community-property jurisdictions. The distinction between community- and common-law states is important whenever death or divorce occur.

Community property (c/p) includes everything that you acquire while you are married and reside in one of the seven community property states. It includes all assets, income, salary, personal possessions, and real estate of both spouses.

Marriage in a community property state means that assets or money earned or received by *either* spouse during marriage is owned equally by each spouse. Items acquired by gift or inheritance are considered the separate property of that spouse. Gifts and bequeaths retain their separate property identity unless the person receiving the gift, known as the *donee*, decides to make a gift of the asset to the other spouse or to the community.

As you will saw under a previous section titled "A Step-Up in Basis," community property offers a tremendous tax advantage not found with other forms of ownership; but this benefit comes at a cost. Under community-property laws, either spouse can sell, transfer, bequest, or gift her or his share without the permission of the other spouse. You may own an asset as community property with your spouse and discover that upon that spouse's death his or her share has been left to someone other than you. In a community property state, the decendent's will may say that a secret boyfriend is to receive her share of the community property; this could not happen with jtwros.

Tenancy by the Entirety

Tenancy by the entirety is a form of joint ownership, except that it involves a husband and wife. It can only be terminated by the joint agreement of both spouses. This form of co-ownership is often used by married couples in separate property states (*see "Community Property" earlier to determine if you live in a separate-property state*).

Custodial Accounts

Accounts set up for minor children or mentally incapacitated people must name a custodian. This is because these categories of people are not considered to have "legal capacity" and therefore, cannot normally enter into a binding contract. Only the custodian can trade, buy, or sell assets in the custodial account. Title to these accounts is usually taken as "Mary Smith, custodian for the benefit of (abbreviated as FBO) Jeff Jones." Even though Jeff Jones is the owner, he lacks legal capacity, either because of age or mental condition. It is for this reason that only Mary Smith, the custodian listed on the account, can make decisions concerning the asset.

Custodians are similar to trustees in that they are overseeing an account, asset, or property for the benefit of another individual, group or entity. In the case of a trust, the trustee is also often the trustor (the person who created the trust).

Custodial accounts are most frequently found with minor children. Once a child becomes an adult, the custodian's name is dropped from the account and the 18 year old (age 21 in some states) is free to do whatever she or he wants with the account. Custodian accounts are usually part of a guardianship or conservatorship.

Partnerships

Any two or more adults may enter into a partnership. A partnership has some common business goal. There are two types of partners: general and limited. The general partners are responsible for the day-to-day operations of the partnership. The general partners are fully liable for any claims against the partnership.

Limited partners have limited rights and therefore limited liability. A limited partner is not liable for the losses, debts, or lawsuits incurred by the partnership. Limited partners can lose their entire investment in the partnership, but no more. The only way a limited partner may be liable for more than his or her contribution to the partnership is if they signed a note or got a letter of credit. Sometimes a limited partner is found to have been so active in the partnership that they are deemed to be a general partner.

Corporations

A corporation can be created by one or more individuals. Corporations are usually formed to limit one's liability. It is commonly believed that in the event of a lawsuit or claim, only the assets of the corporation are at risk. This is often not true. A corporation will not protect the personal assets of a corporate officer or employee who is accused of fraud or an intentional act such as slander or bodily harm. Furthermore, the "corporate veil" will not protect someone who uses the corporation as their alter ego. It is not very common that a court will protect the personal assets of someone just because she or he has a personal corporation.

Until a few years ago, corporate tax brackets used to be lower than individual rates. This has all changed; corporate rates are now higher than individual rates. For the privilege of being a corporation, franchise tax fees must be paid annually and corporate tax returns filed each year for the state and the federal government. Accounting and tax preparation fees are usually higher than those charged for individuals and couples. This is yet another reason why most people should avoid the corporate status.

Trusts

Accounts and property that are part of a trust must name one or more trustees. Only the trustee has the right to manage, buy, or sell assets within the trust. Trust accounts are easy to identify; title to the account is something like "Ursel Jones, trustee of the Jones Family Trust." The person who creates the trust, known as the *trustor* or *trust maker*, can change trustees at anytime. People who create trusts usually name themselves as the trustee.

Assets placed within a trust maintain their original identity; all separate property remains under the sole ownership of one person. Jointly held property (tenancy in common, jtwros, c/p, tenancy by the entirety) also keeps its co-owner status. These distinctions are normally only important if there is a divorce or death.

Summary

As you have now seen, there are several ways to own property. How your assets are titled can cost or save you a great deal of money in the event of a divorce or death. The amount of income tax liability or tax write-offs that you can get depends on four things:

1. If there was a death before the sale.
2. How was the property titled just before it was sold.
3. The selling price.
4. The adjusted basis (cost) of the asset.

When computing estate taxes, the title of the asset and its fair market value on the date of death are the two deciding factors.

Before you go out and re-title your assets into community property or joint tenancy, bear in mind two points. First, any name change will only have a bearing if the property is sold after death, for estate tax purposes and in the event of a divorce. Second, the potential tax savings may be small in comparison to what would happen if there were a divorce. That is, there is little satisfaction in minimizing taxes if you now only own part of the asset due to a divorce settlement. Therefore, you should only consider a name change from separate property to some form of co-ownership or from joint tenancy to community property if you trust your mate completely.

The proper way to open up an account at a brokerage firm or bank has far greater ramifications than whether you get a 2% or 20% rate of return. Yet, this is something that is rarely written about in investment or financial planning books or magazines.

Understanding how to title your accounts is a necessary part of investing.

13

Asset Mix Worksheet

THERE IS MORE THAN ONE method to determine which investments (and the weighting given to each category) to include in your portfolio. The information in this chapter is a slightly edited version of the very popular T. Rowe Price *Asset Mix Worksheet* . To request an unedited version of this worksheet or information on one or more of the T. Rowe Price mutual funds, call (800) 638-5660 or write:

T. Rowe Price
100 East Pratt Street
Baltimore, Maryland 21202.

Introduction

What should you look for in an investment? Are the investments you have now the right ones for you? How can you reduce your overall investment risk? Your investment program should be carefully constructed to achieve your goals, without taking more risk than you can afford or are comfortable with.

The worksheet guides you, step by step, through the important questions you should ask whenever you choose a new investment or review the ones you already have:

- What financial goals do I want to achieve?
- When do I hope to reach them?
- How much money will I need to invest to achieve my goals?
- How bold or cautious do I want to be in my investments?

When you finish this worksheet, you should have the basic information you need to evaluate your current investments and start planning your strategy for the future.

Step 1: Define Your Financial Goals

Your choice of investments should always be driven by what you want your money to do for you, and when. So the first step in evaluating your portfolio is to clearly identify your financial goals.

You may want your investments to fill specific needs, such as buying a house or car, paying college costs, or helping to supplement your retirement income. Or, your goals may be more general—building up cash reserves or accumulating wealth. Either way, spending some time to determine your objectives will help you to choose the most appropriate investments.

The next step is to identify the approximate time frame for achieving the goals you have just listed. For example, do you want to buy a house in five years, or retire in 20 years? Will your eldest child enter college in nine years?

Setting time horizons for your goals is critical. Why? Because different time horizons require different investment strategies. The sooner you need to spend the money that is now invested, the greater your need to invest for principal stability and liquidity. Conversely, the longer you can leave your money invested, the less you need to worry about short-term price fluctuations, and the more you can focus on earning a high return over time.

Risk, return, and timing are all related. Generally, the riskier an investment, the higher its potential return over time and the more suitable it is for an investor with a longer-term horizon.

Use Chart 1 to indicate your major goals, the estimated cost of each, and when you want to achieve them, for example, in the short term (within two years), intermediate term (three to five years), or long term (beyond five years).

Remember that building and maintaining cash reserves must be classified as a short-term goal even if you want to have the reserves for many years, because only the shortest-term investments supply the necessary stability and liquidity. Also, the chart subdivides the Long-Term category into two time periods, since it could include substantial sums needed for college costs, for example, as well as capital for a more distant retirement date. However, you may treat it as a single category if you prefer.

Chart 1: Define Your Financial Goals

Goal	Short-Term (0–2 yrs)	Intermediate-Term (3–5 yrs)	Long-Term (6–10 yrs)	Long-Term (over 10 yrs)
Cash reserves	$	$	$	$
Major purchase: house, car, etc.				
School or college expenses				
Retirement				
Other				
Total	$____ (A)	$____ (B)	$____ (C)	$____ (D)

Step 2: Check Your Asset Mix

How well do your investments fit your goals and their respective horizons?

Chart 2 can help you evaluate your investments. On the left, write the total projected future costs of your goals (amounts A, B, C, and D from Chart 1) next to their respective time-horizon boxes.

Next, read the most appropriate investment characteristics for each time period and which investments have these characteristics. No investment offers everything, and trade-offs must be made. (Hence, the saying "There is no free lunch.") The trade-offs list the potential drawbacks of each type of investment.

In the far right column of Chart 2, list for each broad time category your current investments and their approximate value. This allows you to compare what you already own with the recommended types of short-, intermediate-, and long-term investments. Remember to include bank accounts, mutual funds, individual stock and bond holding, and all IRAs and other retirement accounts.

You should have assets in each time horizon for which you have a goal, in addition to some money in short-term investments for emergencies. If you have some gaps, you may want to realign the investments you're holding now. Also, check that your investments are appropriate for your objectives. Investments that are much shorter or longer than your goals indicate potential problems. For example, if you are using short-term investments to meet long-term goals, you are probably earning too low a return on your money and your goals may not be met. The same holds true if your investments have longer time horizons than your goals, because your risk may be too high for the goal you wish to achieve.

Chart 2: Check Your Asset Mix

Time Horizon	Amount Needed	Current Investments
Short-term (0–2 years)	$______ (A)	______ $______ ______ $______ ______ $______ ______ $______ ______ $______ Total (E) $______

Investment Characteristics to Look For

- Conservative investments—price doesn't change at all or only changes slightly
- Maturity of no more than two years
- Regular income payments
- Easy access to money; no withdrawal penalties

Trade-Offs

- Lower overall returns
- Vulnerable to inflation

Appropriate Investments

- Money market funds
- CDs or bank deposits
- Short-term notes or bonds
- Adjustable-rate mortgage securities

Time Horizon	Amount Needed	Current Investments	
Intermediate-term (3–5 years)	$________ (B)	________	$________
		________	$________
		________	$________
		________	$________
		________	$________
		Total (F)	$________

Investment Characteristics to Look For

- Moderately aggressive investments—higher income or appreciation potential
- Regular income payments
- Price that moves within a fairly narrow range
- Bonds: maturity of less than five years, or flexibility to shorten maturities

Trade-Offs

- Greater price fluctuation than short-term investments
- Lower returns than more aggressive investments
- Bonds vulnerable to inflation

Appropriate Investments

- Bonds with intermediate maturities
- GNMAs
- Preferred stocks and high-yielding common stocks

Time Horizon	Amount Needed	Current Investments	
Long-term (6–10 years)	$______ (C)	______	$______
		______	$______
		______	$______
		______	$______
		______	$______
		Total (G)	$______

Time Horizon	Amount Needed	Current Investments	
Long-term (over 10 years)	$______ (D)	______	$______
		______	$______
		______	$______
		______	$______
		______	$______
		Total (H)	$______

Investment Characteristics to Look For

- Aggressive investments—history of high yields or high returns over time
- Capital growth potential
- Returns that consistently outpace inflation
- Maturity on investment horizon of at least five years

Trade-Offs

- Potentially high price volatility
- May be less liquid

Appropriate Investments

- Long-term bonds
- Common stocks, especially growth stock
- Real estate (investment property only)
- Foreign securities

Step 3: Compare Your Investments with Your Goals

Can you achieve your goals with the amounts you already have invested? Chart 3 allows you to calculate how much you would need to invest to reach goals that occur in approximately 2, 5, 10, or 20 years. (Specific time periods must be used here instead of a range of years in order to apply specific growth and investment factors.)

For each time horizon, fill in the amount you currently have invested (amounts E, F, G, and H from Chart 2).

Multiply each of these amounts by the growth factor indicated to see what your current investments could be worth in the future, assuming in each case an eight percent, pre-tax annual return.

Now fill in amounts, A, B, C, and D and subtract to find the difference (if any) between the estimated future value of your investments and the amounts you will actually need.

Since a regular investment schedule is generally the most effective and least painful way to save, you can also use Chart 3 to find out how to bridge any differences between your current investments and future needs. Just divide the shortfall by the monthly investment factor.

If you have enough to meet your goals, you're in good shape. But if you're like the most of us, your current investments probably fall short. Most people understand their need for capital, and you need to spend some time researching how much it will take to achieve your goals.

Chart 3: Compare Your Investments with Your Goals

Time Horizon	Current Investments	Growth Factor	Assets Would Grow To	Amount I Need For My Goals	Shortfall (or excess)	Monthly Investment Factor	Monthly Investment Needed
Short-term (2 yrs)	$_____ (E)	X 1.2 =	$_____	$_____ (A)	$_____	÷ 26.1 =	$_____
Intermediate-term (5 yrs)	$_____ (F)	X 1.5 =	$_____	$_____ (B)	$_____	÷ 74.0 =	$_____
Long-term (10 yrs)	$_____ (G)	X 2.2 =	$_____	$_____ (C)	$_____	÷ 184.2 =	$_____
Long-term (20 yrs)	$_____ (H)	X 4.7 =	$_____	$_____ (D)	$_____	÷ 592.9 =	$_____

Factors reflect an hypothetical eight percent pre-tax return, compounded monthly.

Chart 4 provides further information to help you plan now for future needs by showing how regular monthly investments of $50, $200, or $500 can accumulate over various time spans. A convenient way to save regularly is through automatic investment plans, such as regular payroll deductions or transfers from your checking account to an investment such as a mutual fund. These plans not only remove the temptation to spend money you need to save but also, through dollar-cost averaging, reduce the possibility that you might invest a large sum at an historically high price. This strategy does not guarantee that you will always have profits or will avoid losses. Over the long run, however, it can provide attractive returns.

Step 4: Think About Your Personal Tolerance for Risk

To set an investment course that you'll be comfortable following—and won't abandon prematurely—you need to consider your own attitude toward risk.

Chart 4: Use the Power of Compounding

Monthly Investment Amounts	5 years	10 years	20 years	30 years
$50	$3,698	$9,208	$29,647	$75,015
$200	$14,793	$36,833	$118,589	$300,059
$500	$36,983	$92,083	$296,474	$750,148

Chart 5 can help you define your risk profile. Read over the general descriptions of a conservative, moderate, and aggressive investor and compare them with your own investment approach to find the one you most resemble. This can give you further guidance when you go to select investments, although your principal focus should always be on your financial goal.

For example, in selecting intermediate-term investments, a conservative investor might stick largely to fixed-income securities, concentrating on high-quality debt obligations of well-established companies and securities that should be relatively stable in price. Stocks would represent a relatively small percent of assets and might consist of companies paying high dividends. A moderate investor would probably increase the emphasis on stocks, perhaps by investing in a well-diversified growth stock mutual fund. An aggressive investor, in contrast, might select lower-quality, fixed-income investments to maximize yield, and allocate a larger portion of assets to stocks.

To structure a portfolio for long-term investments, a conservative investor should allocate more to stocks than bonds, but might avoid the most volatile market sectors—emerging growth stocks in the US and abroad. A moderate investor could have a modest position in these stocks, while an aggressive investor—prepared to ride out the inevitable ups and downs—might have a more substantial position. On the fixed-income side, a conservative investor would stick to the highest-quality bonds, while the more adventurous might allocate some money to high-yield bonds.

Step 5: Diversify to Reduce Risk

Even if you are an aggressive investor, you want to sleep at night. Whatever your personal-risk profile, one of the best ways to reduce your overall risk is to diversify your investments. This means including a variety of assets that react differently to market conditions. That way, if one investment goes down, it can be balanced by others that remain stable or go up.

If you have a mixture of short- and long-term goals, you will achieve some diversification just by matching your investments to your goals. Another type of diversification involves owning different types of investments within each time category. For example, you could combine stocks and bonds in the intermediate- and long-term categories, or US securities in any category, and so on.

Chart 5: Assess Your Personal Risk Tolerance

- I am a **conservative investor.** I am not comfortable with price volatility. I am willing to give up higher rates of return in order to have this stability. I'm satisfied to earn about 5% to 7% a year—or 1% to 2% more than the inflation rate.
- I am a **moderate investor.** I expect that the value of my investments will fluctuate, but not too drastically. I'd like to earn 8% to 10% a year on average. Some years I might earn more, and some years less.
- I am an **aggressive investor.** My investment may go up and down just as the stock market does. While some years I might have a loss, over time I expect my assets to grow much more than 10% a year, putting me far ahead of inflation.

Step 6: Rethink Your Investments Periodically

It's a good idea to review your goals and investments once a year, and keep your objectives in mind each time you make a new investment. As your circumstances change, you may also want to change your strategy. In the end, all the principles boil down to three simple rules:

1. Set clear financial goals.
2. Choose investments that provide the combination of risk, reward, and time horizon appropriate for you.
3. Minimize your risk by diversifying as broadly as you can.

It takes some time and thought to evaluate your finances, but hopefully, you will agree the results are worth the effort.

The next, and final chapter of the book brings together the information you have learned in the previous chapters. This "cap stone" chapter will aid you in developing a portfolio of investments that gives you the best possible *risk-adjusted* returns. You will learn how you can greatly reduce risk by combining the right investments and by letting time work on your behalf.

14

Modern Portfolio Theory

LET US BEGIN with an overview of modern portfolio theory (MPT), sometimes referred to as *asset allocation.* MPT will give you a good idea as to which types of investments you should be considering and why; by narrowing the selection process you will be saving time and minimizing any confusion. This will give you a real sense of direction. It is also the best defense you have under a Clinton Administration that may not turn out as you suspect, for better or worse.

Modern portfolio theory is the process of distributing portfolio investments among the various available investment categories—money market instruments, bonds, stocks, real estate, and other assets. The asset allocation decision, or the *investment policy decision* as it is also called, actually involves two decisions. First, it involves what assets will be included or excluded from your portfolio. Most individuals are willing to include the conventional classes of money market funds, bonds, and stocks, but more thought has to be given to other asset classes such as international securities, real estate, precious metal, limited partnerships, options, and futures. Once you make the decision on which assets to include, the second decision requires setting the portfolio weights for each asset class. That is, what percentage of the portfolio will be invested in each asset class?

The asset allocation decision is the single most important investment decision made in terms of its impact on the long-term results of an investment plan. In a widely quoted study, researchers found that asset allocation strongly dominates market timing and security selection, explaining 94 percent of the variation in total return for 91 large US pension plans. In short, the decision of what assets classes to own and the percentage of the portfolio to be invested in each class totally overwhelms the impact of what particular securities are owned within each asset class. Within the conventional asset classes, for example, the decision to invest 70 percent of a portfolio in a broadly diversified group of common stocks or common stock mutual funds is far more important than the selection of individual stocks or a specific fund in terms of its impact on long-run performances.

Modern portfolio theory takes the art of investing and transforms it into a science. MPT is *the* best way for you to assure that you will get the results you expect within a given time period.

Until recently, MPT was rarely written about and generally only in highly technical books, journals, and papers. The software needed for MPT was quite costly, ranging anywhere from $50,000 to $200,000 *annually*. In the past, only large money managers could afford this program. Today, modern portfolio theory has gained greater publicity and the software costs are generally less than $2,000 per year.

This method of investing has been around for close to 40 years, yet few stockbrokers or financial planners understand how it works. According to *Money Magazine*, asset allocation is "the most valuable secret in investing today." Coincidentally, the founders of MPT are recent Nobel Peace Prize winners in Economics. These two men, Markovitz and Sharpe, were honored because of their work in MPT. The theory has clearly demonstrated its value and forecasting abilities over the past several decades. But, you may ask, "What does this have to do with me?"

Well, if you are like most people who are investing for their future, you believe that *which* stocks, bonds, real estate or tangibles you buy will be the deciding factor in determining how big your nest egg will grow. What will surprise you is that *nothing could be further from the truth.*

A 1991 study published in the *Financial Analysts Journal* revealed that over 93% of a portfolio's performance has to do with which asset categories are included and what weights are given to each category (for example, X% in tax-free bonds, Y% in global government bonds, and Z% in real estate). Timing, when to go into the market or get out of it, and individual security selection (for example, Apple or IBM stock) account for the other 6–7%. A 1989 article in *Equity International*, a magazine written for money managers around the world, states that, "Asset mix represents no less than 94% of performance… just 3% comes from picking the right security… The other 3% comes from timing." And finally, the often quoted *Stocks, Bonds, Bills & Inflation: 1990 Yearbook* points out: "There is only a 1% correlation between the performance of stocks from one year to the next and only a 9% correlation for government bonds."

Modern portfolio theory is just as important for those in their thirties as it is for an individual or couple in their sixties or seventies. Yet, it does not have to be complicated. Simply stated, we are finding out how much money, or what percentage of our holdings, should be placed in what category. MPT assumes that investors prefer to have portfolios that offer either less risk at the same level of reward or more reward at one's existing level of risk.

MPT: Three Parts

There are three components to modern portfolio theory:

- Historical returns
- Standard deviation
- Correlation coefficients.

Historical returns simply shows how each of several dozen investment categories (such as blue chip stocks, gold, residential real estate, growth funds, and so on) have performed in the past. Obviously, all other things being equal (which they rarely are), the higher the return, the better. Usually the most recent 10–20 year period of time is used for purposes of expected (or projected) rates of return for the future.

Standard deviation shows how volatile an investment has been over the past 36 months. Intuitively, you and I know that some investments go up and down more often and to a greater degree than others. Blue chip stocks, for example, are more volatile than money market funds or tax-free bonds. The greater the volatility, the higher the standard deviation. In most cases, the greater the volatility, the riskier the investment. A common goal of investors is to get the highest return possible with the least amount of corresponding risk.

Correlation coefficients show how two investments "interact" with each other. That it, some investments have a tendency to move up and down together at about the same degree and at about the same time. Such investments are *positively correlated.* An example of this is US government bonds and corporate bonds. When two investments move in a random fashion, they are *randomly correlated.* This means that when one moves up, down, or remains unchanged in value, the other may do nothing, the same thing, or the opposite. How it will react is not really known, until after the fact. A good example of this is US stocks and foreign stocks. When two investments move in an opposite direction at about the same time, they are *negatively correlated.* An example of this is money market funds and long-term government or corporate bonds. When interest rates go up, so do yields and returns on money market funds, but the value of corporate, government (and often municipal) bonds goes down.

Models show that investors can optimize their risk/return combinations by investing in what are called *efficient portfolios.* An efficient portfolio provides the highest possible return at each risk level. Return and risk go hand-in-hand, resulting in the familiar risk/return trade-off curve that shows return increasing as risk increases. According to MPT, an efficient portfolio is decided upon by expected future returns, standard deviations of returns and correlations of returns for different asset classes.

Getting the Best Risk-Adjusted Return: The Efficient Frontier

An efficient portfolio is one that has the highest possible expected return, given its risk. On the chart, the efficient frontier is shown by the curve labeled AB. When plotted with risk on the horizontal axis and return on the vertical axis, curve AB represents the highest possible return for each level of risk.

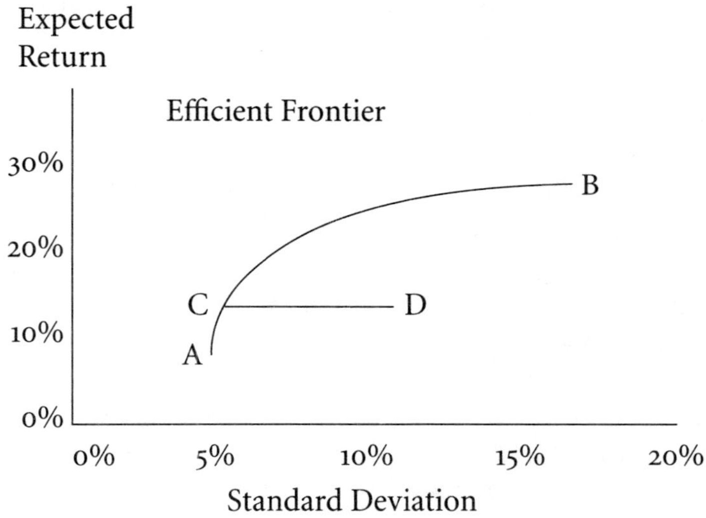

A, B, and C=Efficient Portfolios
D=Sub-obtimal Portfolio

As an example, note point D on the graph. Whereas point D has an expected return of 12%, it has an associated risk of 11% (as measured in standard deviation). Note that point C, along the efficient frontier, also has an expected return of 12%. Its standard deviation, however, is only 5%. For an expected return of 12%, a rational investor would never choose the portfolio with a standard deviation of 11% when 5% is available. Thus, portfolio D is inefficient. The chart depicts three hypothetical portfolios that are efficient (A, B, and C) and one that is not (D).

How Investments Interact: Correlation Coefficient

The correlation coefficient measures the degree to which the returns on two assets move together. If they move in exactly lock step, they are said to be perfectly positively correlated; their correlation coefficient is +1.0. If they move exactly the *opposite* of each other, their correlations is –1.0. If there is no relationship at all, the correlation is 0.0 (actually, a *random* correlation exists if the number ranges between –0.3 and +0.3). The "magic of diversification" is that if assets with low correlations are grouped together in portfolios, the overall variability of the portfolio is reduced.

Consider an extreme case where two assets both have an average annual return of 10 percent, an annual standard deviation of 20 percent, and a correlation of –1.0. A correlation of –1.0 means the returns (or movements in price) on the two assets are exactly the opposite of each other. Both average 10 percent per year in return, but when one is up, the other is down and vice versa. If the two assets are combined into a portfolio in equal amounts, the portfolio would average 10 percent per year, but have a standard deviation of zero; meaning *no risk*. The two individual assets would have up years and down years, but *together* would earn 10 percent every year.

Of course, perfect negative correlation does not happen in the real world, but asset classes do have correlations of less than one and are sometimes negative. MPT shows the combination of assets that yield the maximized expected return at each level of risk (standard deviation). The graph of all points is called the efficient frontier.

Most large pension funds and endowment funds that are professionally managed use some variation of MPT to determine their optimal asset allocation. They look at the efficient frontier that is available to them from the asset categories they are considering, and decide where they want to be located on the efficient frontier. Specifically, they first decide how much or how little risk they are willing to accept; something that should also be your first concern when structuring a portfolio for retirement. Locating the efficient frontier is actually the easiest part of the exercise.

At first glance, most people would look at the following table and think that investing is simple; invest everything in common and small stocks. Why accept a 9.4% return from government bonds when you could get 17.3% per year from an aggressive growth mutual fund? Before you rush out and start playing the market, look at the right-hand column that measures risk. It shows how volatile each of these investments have been over the past 15 years. Notice the large standard deviations investors have experienced with stocks. As with other things in life, investing is a trade-off. If you seek higher returns then you must accept greater risk.

The figures from this table are historical, covering the past 15 years (through 3/92), and are not the same rates of return shown in the previous chapter. The figures below are from RAMCAP (telephone (303) 750-5535), a software company that specializes in MPT software.

Asset Category	Average Annual Return	Standard Deviation
Cash Equivalents	7.2	0.7
Large Stocks	12.0	16.9
Small Stocks	15.0	22.8
Real Estate	11.4	5.7
Oil and Gas	9.1	19.1
Leasing	11.0	4.4
Intermediate Term Government Bonds	9.4	11.2
Annuity (Fixed-Rate)	10.0	1.0
Balanced Fund	12.7	10.3
Convertible Bond Fund	12.0	9.9
Corporate High-Yield Fund	10.6	8.2
Government Bond Fund	9.0	5.7
Growth Fund	15.2	15.4
Growth and Income Fund	13.9	13.4
International Bond Fund	13.2	9.1
International Stock Fund	15.3	14.0
Municipal Bond Fund	6.4	7.4
Municipal Bond High-Yield Fund	7.5	7.7
Small Company Growth Fund	19.1	20.0
Aggressive Growth Fund	17.3	20.0

As you can see, as the risk of an investment increases, so does the possibility of a loss. For example, in the past, large (blue chip) stocks have compounded at an average annual return of 12%, but over any given *year*, such returns could have been as high as 45.8% and as low as –21.8% (to calculate the range of return for any investment, take its average annual rate of return and add to it, or subtract from it, the standard deviation multiplied by two). Suddenly, common stocks may no longer have the same appeal. The typical investor would not consider any investment in which he or she could lose as much as 22% in a single year. Fortunately, there is a way to reduce such volatility—"time diversification."

Lengthen the Period, Reduce the Risk

Notice that the previous section discussed the standard deviation (volatility) over a one-year period. This kind of risk can be greatly reduced when longer periods of time are used. The next series of charts shows how returns become more predictable, and positive, the longer the holding period. Average returns may change little, if any, but volatility drops by quite a bit. You have now learned the first lesson about successful investing: Time is one way to reduce risk.

As an example, the risk associated with holding common stocks can be significantly reduced by adopting longer investment holding periods. This means two things to you:

- The sooner you begin planning for retirement, the greater the universe of investments you will have to choose from, since many volatile investments become quite stable as the holding period is extended.
- The ultimate outcome of your portfolio's overall return becomes more predictable.

To understand this principle, consider the historical performance of common stocks over the last 50 years (1942–1991). The chart that follows shows a series of vertical bars. Each bar represents a range of returns for a given investment holding period.

The far-left bar shows the historical performance for one-year holding periods. The best one-year period (for common stocks) between 1942 and 1991 provided a return of 53%. The worst one-year period provided a return of –26%. The average was 14%. The other bars show the historical performance for 3-year, 5-year, 10-year, 15-year and 20-year holding periods. The best 20-year period provided an annualized return of 17%, while the worst 20-year period provided an annualized return of 7%. The average was 11%. Notice that as the investment period lengthens, the historical range of returns narrows. Thus, the longer the investment time period, the more attractive and predictable common stocks become.

The following six charts show the historical return ranges for common stocks, small stocks, intermediate-term government bonds, long-term government bonds, corporate bonds, and T-bills.

Common Stock Return Range 1941–1991

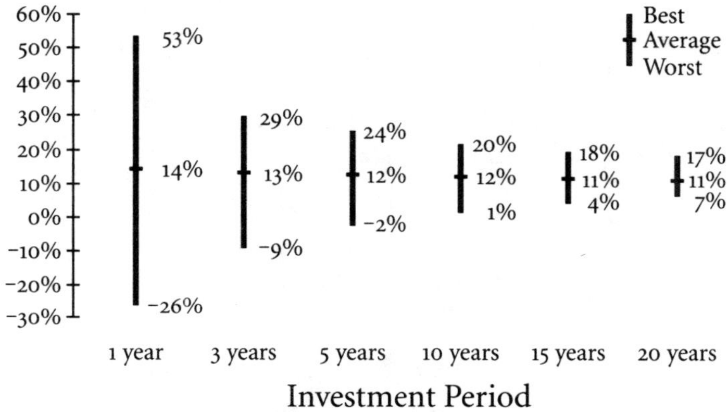

Small Stock Return Range 1941–1991

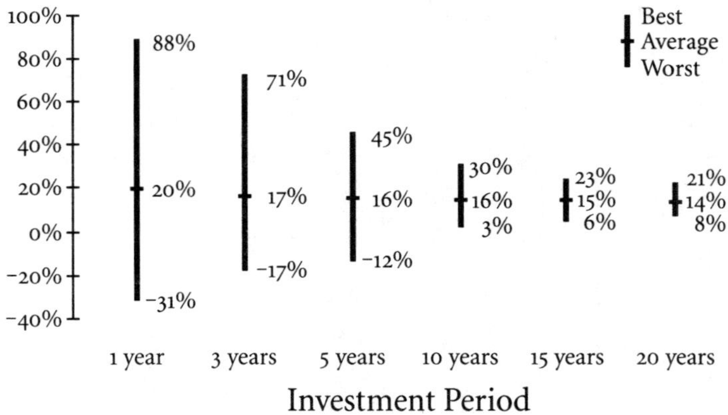

Intermediate-Term Government Bond Return Range 1941–1991

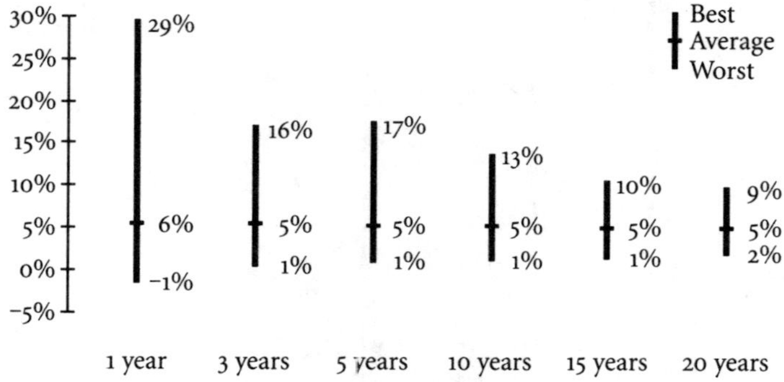

Investment Period

Long-Term Government Bond Return Range 1941–1991

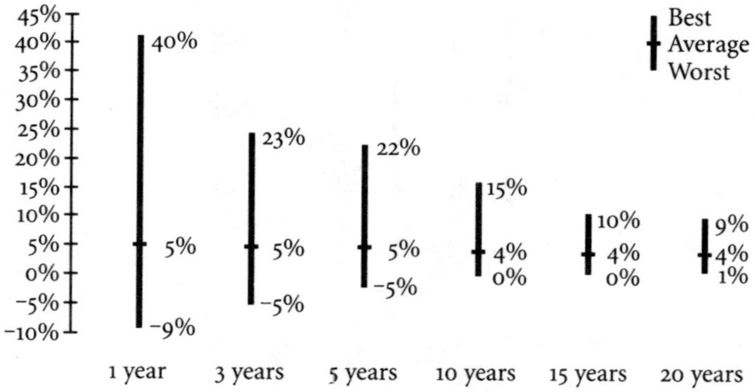

Investment Period

Corporate Bond Return Range 1941–1991

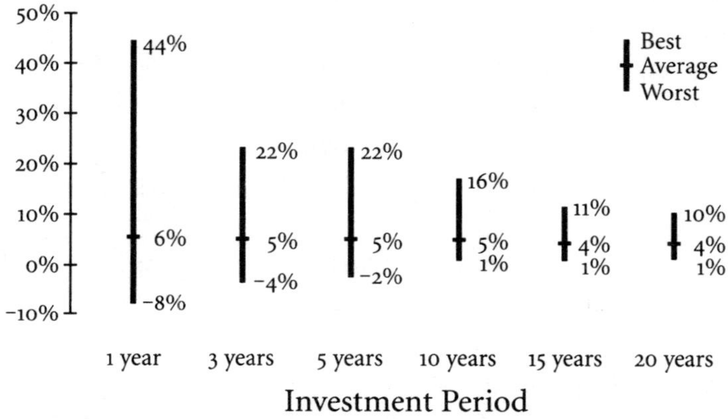

Treasury Bill Return Range 1941–1991

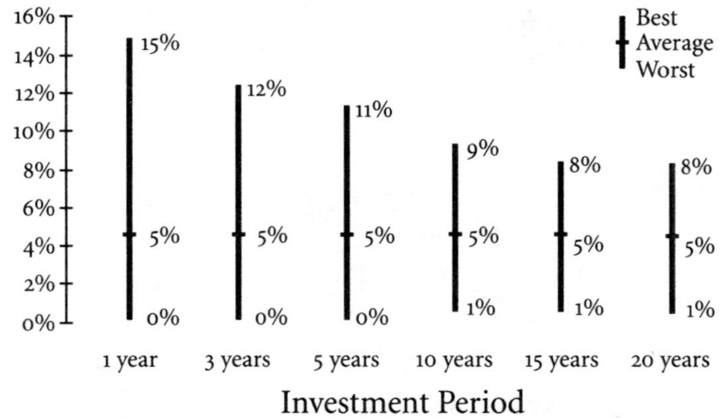

Another way to reduce risk is by investing in several different categories. All investments do not go up and down together. A drop in the stock market may mean a rally in government bonds. Owning several different stocks from different countries and industries will make you less susceptible to the policies of one corporation or nation. The risk of owning real estate is lowered by owning different types of real estate in more than one area. A recession or business slowdown in one state does not necessarily mean tough times in another part of the nation.

According to modern portfolio theory, the impact of a particular security on the overall portfolio depends on its return, its risk, and the movement of it in relation to others, known as *covariance.* Although it may seem odd, the addition of a risky security may make the overall portfolio less risky, maybe even more so than by adding a conservative security (assuming the risky investment is *negatively* correlated to the rest of the portfolio). On the other hand, if it has the same covariance as the others, it does little to reduce risk.

MPT Worksheet Printout

The following table shows how a portfolio can be improved by taking advantage of the knowledge afforded by MPT. A simple repositioning, when done in the right proportions, can actually increase one's return and reduce overall risk. The categories selected and the percentage figures used are from an MPT software program. To learn more about this type of software, contact an investment advisor or broker who has the designation CFS (Certified Fund Specialist). If you cannot find a CFS in your area, telephone 1-800-848-2029. This is the telephone number of the Institute of Certified Fund Specialists; they will refer you to a CFS nearby.

Risk Return Comparison Analysis

Asset Description	Proposed Asset Allocation	Current Allocation
Cash Equivalents	0%	20%
Domestic Equities	5%	20%
Large Stocks	5%	40%
Small Stocks	7%	20%
International Equities	10%	0%
Real Estate	25%	0%
Domestic Bonds	13%	0%
Foreign Bonds	13%	0%
Balanced Index	7%	0%
Leasing	15%	0%
Total	**100%**	**100%**

	Proposed	Current
Average Rate of Return	12%	11%
Average Variation	11%	27%
Probability of Loss	2% (1 in 48)	20% (1 in 5)
Average Recovery Time (if there were a loss)	Less than One Month	More than 16 Months

Probability of Losing Purchasing Power	Proposed	Current
Over 1 year	12% (1 in 9)	32% (1 in 3)
Over 5 years	0.5% (1 in 263)	15% (1 in 7)

Expected Range of Returns	Proposed	Current
1 Year Range	0.5%–23.5%	–16%–39%
3 Year Range	5%–19%	–4%–27%
5 Year Range	7%–17%	–1%–24%
10 Year Range	8%–16%	3%–10%
15 Year Range	9%–15%	5%–19%

Dollar Growth of Portfolio	Proposed	Current
1 Year Cumulative Growth	$112,000	$112,000
3 Year Cumulative Growth	$140,000	$139,000
5 Year Cumulative Growth	$176,000	$172,000
10 Year Cumulative Growth	$310,000	$297,000
15 Year Cumulative Growth	$547,000	$513,000

Proposed portfolio will increase the mean return by 4%.

Proposed portfolio will decrease variability (risk) by 58%.

Proposed portfolio is 10 times less likely to lose principal.

As you can see, MPT can have a dramatic effect on the return of a portfolio and its level of risk. Unfortunately, only a small percentage of financial advisors understand or use MPT.

You now know the basics of asset allocation: return, risk, and diversification. The proper understanding of these basics can result in predictable returns and the fulfillment of your financial goals. Let us now turn to a *specific* form of MPT, *strategic asset allocation.* This next section will help clarify what you have just learned about MPT *plus* show you another way to reduce risk—through "time diversification."

Strategic Asset Allocation

Asset allocation is a modern day financial buzzword. It appears as if everyone is an asset allocator these days. Those who manage balanced mutual funds (that is, funds that invest in a combination of common stocks and bonds) now refer to themselves as *asset allocators.* Market timers, those people who attempt to gain an investment advantage by investing in common stocks when prices are rising, and investing in money market funds when stock prices are expected to fall, also refer to themselves as asset allocators. Even institutional money managers who practice highly active trading strategies, such as program trading or portfolio insurance, have adopted the phrase *asset allocation* to describe their investment practices. In fact, asset allocation has been used as an umbrella to cover many diverse investment strategies. The approach that appears to have been the most successful over the past several dozen years, both in academic and investment circles, is what is referred to as *strategic asset allocation.*

Strategic asset allocation refers to the practice of diversifying capital across many investment classes with the goal of constructing optimal portfolios of assets (what is referred to earlier as the *efficient frontier*). That is, strategic asset allocation is an attempt to construct the lowest risk portfolio that will still deliver an investor's required rate of return. At the core of strategic asset allocation is the relationship of investment returns among the various categories of assets contained in a widely diversified portfolio.

Generally, strategic asset allocation is a passive or semi-active strategy. It is a passive strategy because instead of attempting to second guess the market (that is, to allocate capital on the basis of short-term forecasts of market direction), strategic asset allocators maintain a posture of being invested in diverse categories of assets at all times. The strategy is semi-active because portfolio managers periodically re-balance the portfolio back to the initial allocation percentages.

To illustrate the appeal of strategic asset allocation, let us examine one of the darkest hours in our financial history—the period 1929 through 1932. During this four-year period, common stock investors who maintained a fully invested posture in a diversified portfolio of blue chip common stocks (such as the Standard & Poor's 500 Index) saw the value of their portfolios decline by an average of 64%. This same portfolio did not fully recover its losses until 1936. On the other hand, an investor who held a portfolio containing equal investments in common stocks, long-term government bonds, and Treasury Bills and re-balanced this portfolio at the end of each year would have suffered a 19% decline. In addition, this loss would have been entirely erased *the next year* (1933). Furthermore, considering the fact that consumer prices declined by 24% during the four years, 1929–32, this investor's real wealth would have actually *increased* during one of the most turbulent financial periods in our history.

Consider a snapshot of more recent history. Namely, the period encompassing the stock market meltdown during October 1987. The year 1987 was an investment roller coaster that most investors will never forget. The year began with the Dow Jones Industrial Average below the 2000 level. By mid-August, it had risen above 2700. However, during one hectic trading day in October, the blue chip average lost more than 500 points. When the smoke had cleared, thousands of individual investors had found that their entire investment stake had been wiped out. Scores of small and medium-sized brokerage firms were driven out of business.

During three months, September through November 1987, the Standard & Poor's 500 Index, a broadly based index of blue chip common stocks, had declined by 29.5%. On the other hand, during these same three months, long-term government bonds appreciated by 2.7 percent and Treasury Bills by 1.5 percent. A portfolio containing equal investments in blue chip stocks, long-term government bonds and Treasury Bills would have declined by only six percent during those three months; by the end of February 1988, these losses would have been entirely eliminated.

The uncertainty of the portfolio is a function of both the risk of the individual assets contained in the portfolio and the correlation of returns between any two or more assets. This is the most important concept in developing strategically allocated portfolios. Portfolio risk can be reduced by combining assets with correlation of returns less than 1.0. In other words, one can reduce investment risk not only by *not* putting all one's eggs in one basket, but by selecting the right kinds of baskets.

As an example, the correlation of return between long-term government bonds and the price of gold is negative. Therefore, a fixed-income investor can decrease the variability (or risk) of a bond portfolio by combining fixed-income investments with an investments in gold bullion. Although gold bullion has historically provided minimal returns (about equal to the rate of inflation) and has a high degree of variability, its negative correlation with long-term domestic bonds makes it an ideal candidate for a conservative investor interested in a fixed-income portfolio.

This, of course, makes a lot of intuitive sense. Interest rates are usually driven upward (and bonds prices are driven downward) during periods of high inflation. However, during these periods the price of gold often rises. Thus, the decrease in fixed-income return, which accompanies a decline in bond prices, is offset by an increase in the price of gold.

An "All Weather" Portfolio

Conside a portfolio containing investment in each of seven classes of assets: blue-chip stocks (the S & P 500), aggressive growth stocks, foreign stocks, gold bullion, long-term government bonds, foreign bonds, and Treasury Bills (or a money market fund). This portfolio is referred to as an "all weather portfolio."

The portfolio is re-balanced to the original allocations at the end of each year (1972–1991). As you can see in the following table, this portfolio produced a total return of 1,108% during the 20-year period. The Standard & Poor's 500 Index, by contrast, provided a total return (capital appreciation plus dividend yield) of 946% during the period. Furthermore, the all weather portfolio declined in value during only two years, with the largest decline, four percent, occurring during 1990.

In contrast, the Standard and Poor's 500 Index (a proxy for the stock market) declined in value during five years with the largest decline, 26%, occurring during 1974. The all weather portfolio provided a greater rate of return than blue chip stocks during the period and experienced far less return variability or investment risk.

All Weather Portfolio Returns

	All 7 Assets	S & P 500	T-Bills	Mix*	All 7 No Gold	All 7 No Gold or Cash	All 7 No Cash
1972	16%	19%	4%	9%	12%	13%	18%
1973	2%	–15%	7%	0%	–8%	–11%	1%
1974	1%	–26%	8%	–3%	–9%	–12%	0%
1975	21%	37%	6%	16%	24%	28%	23%
1976	13%	24%	5%	11%	19%	22%	15%
1977	14%	–7%	5%	1%	13%	15%	15%
1978	17%	7%	7%	7%	15%	16%	19%
1979	19%	18%	10%	13%	12%	12%	20%
1980	31%	32%	11%	18%	19%	21%	34%
1981	–1%	–5%	15%	8%	3%	1%	–4%
1982	16%	21%	11%	14%	18%	20%	17%
1983	13%	23%	9%	13%	17%	18%	13%
1984	2%	6%	10%	9%	5%	4%	1%
1985	28%	32%	8%	16%	31%	36%	32%
1986	26%	18%	6%	10%	27%	31%	30%
1987	11%	5%	5%	5%	10%	11%	12%
1988	10%	17%	6%	10%	14%	16%	11%
1989	10%	31%	9%	16%	12%	13%	11%
1990	–4%	–3%	8%	4%	–4%	–6%	–5%
1991	16%	31%	6%	14%	20%	23%	17%
Total Return							
	1108%	946%	444%	609%	970%	1102%	1266%
Compound Return							
	12.8%	11.9%	7.7%	9.5%	12.0%	12.7%	13.5%

* *Mix = ⅓ stocks (S & P 500) + ⅔ Treasury Bills*

The following bar chart visually depicts possible returns for different holding periods over the past 20 years using the "all weather" portfolio. It can be compared to the charts of individual assets earlier in this chapter. Notice how the loss is much lower (more acceptable) for shorter holding periods.

All Weather Portfolio Return Range 1972–1991

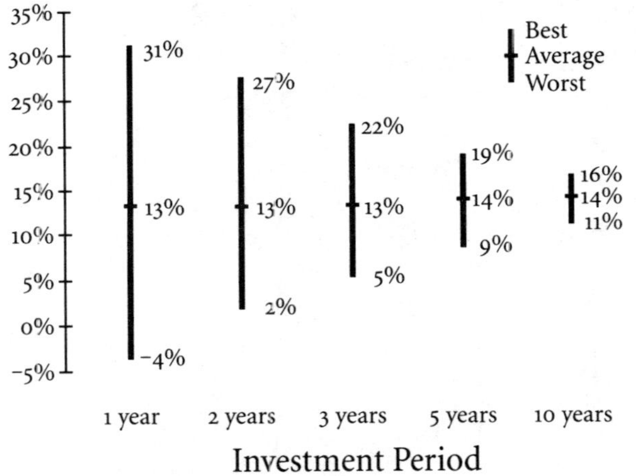

To give you a more precise feel for how risk can be reduced through diversification, look at the next table which shows how predictability of returns is more assured (narrower) when an "all weather" portfolio is used. Also note the far right-hand column of the table, which indicates how *risk-adjusted* return is superior with asset allocation.

Risk and Return

Portfolio	Return	Standard Deviation	Return Per Unit of Risk
S & P 500 Index	13.3%	17.1%	.78
All Weather—7 Assets	13.1%	9.2%	1.42
All Weather—No Gold Or Cash	13.6%	12.7%	1.07
All Weather—No Gold	12.5%	10.5%	1.19
All Weather—No Cash	14.0%	10.9%	1.28

Shortcomings of MPT

Modern portfolio theory is helpful in determining the basic risk-reward relationships using asset category averages. It will *not* help you in determining a specific security selection, such as which common stock is best or what corporate bond fund you should invest in. A money manager or mutual fund advisor's skill in overseeing a certain portfolio is also ignored. MPT will provide you with a framework to work in, showing what categories and the weighting of those categories, depending on the risk one is willing to accept. It should be the basis for deciding which investments are to go into your portfolio, a key aspect of financial planning.

Summary

Too often, investors and brokers spend the great majority of their time trying to pick the next hot mutual fund or stock. Studies clearly show that this has minimal impact on a portfolio's long-term results. A great deal of anguish and thought goes into trying to time the market (that is, when to buy and when to sell). Studies show that not only is this a waste of time, it actually *detracts* from performance. The answer to successful investing is clearly *proper* diversification. Modern portfolio theory (MPT) is helpful in determining the basic risk-reward relationship between two or more investment categories. Understanding such relationships, or correlations, is the key to proper diversification.

The circle is complete. You now know which investments will do well during the Clinton years, a means of structuring a portfolio, and how to determine (through the help of a Certified Fund Specialist or other financial advisor who uses MPT software) which asset categories can give you the best *risk-adjusted* returns. The next step is in your hands. Don't do what most investors do—procrastinate. The Clinton presidency offers tremendous investment opportunities, but you must become active.